THE
SEER'S REALM
OF THE
KINGDOM

THE
SEER'S REALM
OF THE
KINGDOM

By
Dr. Showalter Johnson

DEDICATION

This book is dedicated to my parents.
Fredrick Johnson
and
Miriam Johnson

"See first the Kingdom of God and all jurisdictions will be added unto you."

—*Dr. Showalter Johnson*

CONTENTS

Chapter 1

Since he was a young boy, Mateo has seen the colors swirl above people's heads whenever he played the piano at worship. As he pressed the keys, the music permeated his soul and the transformation inside and outside of him could only be seen and felt by him.

He'd tried many times to tell the elders in the Baptist church, but they'd hear nothing of it. They dismissed him as well as his imagination. How often he met their eyes with hope that they'd listen this time. Maybe the pastor would give him an explanation for the things he saw every time he played the piano.

But the explanations were pedantic and included scoldings about the dangers of the imagination or how the imagination was a tool of Satan or some other pontification that didn't fit at all with what he saw.

To him, what he saw felt like love.

So, he continued for years to worship in the Bahamas at the keyboard in the Baptist churches, usually in a corner of the pulpit next to the drums. Today, like any Sunday, the church was crowded to capacity, and he continued to see the swirling colors around people's heads. He saw angels pass through closed curtains. And he continued to see the highlighted ancient writings that he had come to fondly call the angelic notary.

And today as he played, and he worshipped, and he listened to his fellow parishioners sing, he lifted his eyes to look out over them. And this time, for the second time in his life, he saw a green color hover around a woman's heart. Not the usual reds or blues or scarlets he'd see hovering above. No, this was green. And he knew he had to speak to her. He knew it was his responsibility.

Mateo heard the pastor speak the Aaronic blessings:

"The Lord bless thee and keep thee; the Lord make his face shine upon thee and be gracious unto thee; the Lord lift up his countenance upon thee and give thee peace."

Mateo continued to play as the parishioners rose from their seats. Some mingled a while, chatting with friends. The deacons' wives sat patiently, waiting for their husbands to return from counting the tithes and offerings. Parishioners smiled and thanked the pastor for his sermon. But Mateo kept his eye on the woman, meaning to catch her attention as she passed.

He stopped playing without finishing the song, and the silence was like a hush over the room.

Mateo rose from his piano bench to call out to the woman as she started to walk by.

"Please, madam. May I have a moment of your time?"

The woman smiled nervously and pressed her hand up to her chest.

"Me?"

"Yes, please. I have something important to tell you," Mateo said.

As the parishioners continued to pass by, she stepped up unto the pulpit and tentatively approached Mateo.

"Was it something I sang?" she smiled.

"No, no," Mateo smiled. He extended his hand and said, "My name is Mateo Bethel."

She reached out to shake his hand.

"Oh, yes. I know who you are. Everyone here knows who you are. Your playing speaks for you," she said.

Mateo nodded. Blushed a bit.

"Thank you."

"I'm Ledija Woodside. Nice to meet you."

"I'm sorry to be so matter of fact about this, but I must tell you something very important," Mateo said. "I see. . . "

Mateo caught himself. He didn't want to tell her about everything he was seeing around her heart. The ancient writings. The pretty curved letters. The green color that highlighted her heart, as if a flashlight shone all around it.

Mateo knew this meant she was sick in her heart. He looked away from her brown eyes a moment, the green light flickering across his own eyes.

Ledija tilted her head to catch his eyes again and smiled.

"What is it? What do you see?" she said.

Mateo turned back to her gaze and knew she must be prayed for. He knew he had to tell her.

"I sense . . . I believe that . . . " he struggled. "It is very important that you visit the doctor. I think there is something in your heart that needs a doctor."

"Why? What are you talking about?" Ledija's smile disappeared.

"Please, madam," said Mateo. "I cannot explain. Please. It is very important that you see a doctor right away."

Several church members went about the business of picking up sermons and returning Bibles to their proper places as the few remaining parishioners moved with the line out the intricately stenciled and carved wood doors.

Ledija searched Mateo's face for more answers.

"But, why? Why should I just believe you?" she said. "I mean, I don't believe you. This is really mean. And it's *Sunday*."

"I am sorry. But, please . . . do go. As quickly as possible."

Mateo turned back to his piano and played. He could feel her staring at him, until he heard her heels click the marble as she walked away. He looked after her and watched as she slipped out the door. He prayed for her and returned his focus to his music . . . and to his worship.

Chapter 2

As Mateo played, he couldn't help but recall his journey to get to this place . . . this place, where he could see what others could not see. This place, where he knew and responded in faith and obedience to his father. As a seer he was an ambassador of God's Kingdom, which meant he must intercede in the affairs of nations and people on His behalf and behest.

It is the word of God that "so if you are a seer and a prophet you are called to a nation, not just an individual, giving them a word of comfort, avocation, and exultation because that is a gift of prophecy." The office of a prophet or seer has to do with a nation. And we're not going to be able to deal with a nation if we are still adolescent. This is one of the many reasons we must grow up.

For Mateo, Ledija represented all the times and all the ways he had to take up his responsibility and do what he had to do. He was accustomed to being in places that were not compatible with what he had to say. He'd always hoped that, wherever he went to speak about what he saw, it would be agreed to. Just like that. But no, that's not how it goes. He was sent, just like the prophets before him, to places with people who didn't want to hear and who refused to see . . . but Mateo had to speak anyway, to seek to alter minds, transform people's hearts, and show what is possible in God's Kingdom.

Ledija was just another example of it, in the form of a lovely woman, who he hoped would do what she needed to do to help herself.

Mateo sighed and slammed his fingers across the keys in frustration from years of not being believed, jolting the silence in the room.

Chapter 3

"Excuse me, sir?"

Mateo looked up to see a young male parishioner that he had not seen before. He was a quiet young man and seemed very intense and shy.

"I see it, too," he said.

"See what?" Mateo said.

"The color."

There was reservation in Mateo's voice as he studied the young man's face. "What color are you talking about?"

"I see the green around her heart, sir."

Mateo shot up from his piano bench and stood so tall it was if he were being pulled by a string from above. Mateo searched the young man's face. Their eyes locked.

The young man did not flinch.

"Look," the young man said. "My name is Evan Miller. I see colors above people's heads. But this is the only time I've ever seen such a green light around somebody's heart."

Evan's appearance was not one to inspire confidence in Mateo. His blue jeans sagged low, his high-top sneakers were unlaced, and his Rastafarian T-shirt was faded and barely tucked in. It also had a picture of Bob Marley smoking a joint on the front.

Evan grew impatient.

"Alright, man," he said. "You don't have to believe me either. I'm used to it by now. But I'm telling you, man . . . *I* saw what *you* saw."

Mateo's eyes shone from within.

"Tell me more," said Mateo.

Mateo motioned for the young man to sit down, but he did not. It was as if he'd been held down for so long from speaking that he had to get it all out.

Evan told Mateo of his experience with music. He'd played the slack guitar since he was five or so. He told of the many times he'd seen visions while playing, and the more he tried to explain to his family, the less they understood. They just wanted him to play. And play he did. In fact, he was on the island for a performance. He pulled out his phone and showed Mateo his website.

Mateo saw the face of an artist and an angel in the shy and awkward photos he saw.

"But why are you here?" said Mateo.

"I'm here because I've always promised my parents that I would attend worship. That I should never let my music feed my ego, but recognize it as the gift it is . . . blah blah . . . you know. But, when I'm playing, it's like I feel God's glory. But even that seemed like an egotistical thing when I tried to explain that to my parents or pastors or music teachers or whoever."

Mateo watched as Evan spoke. His face was filled with love and light, but also so much anger and frustration. It reminded him of his own feelings. But Evan's voice was alive with new strength and volume.

"But this is the first time I saw the colors while someone else was playing music. This is the first time I saw them while listening to you."

Mateo's face paled and he turned away from the young man and approached his piano, all the while lifting his face to the light coming through the stenciled windows.

"Can you tell me what it is? Do you know? Can you help me?" Evan pressed.

Mateo opened his piano bench, like any musician who might be pulling out some new sheets of music to play. But when Mateo reached in, he pulled out a folder filled with typed pages . . . crumpled, written on, erased, faded, and a bit turned up and over at the corners. The pages were held together with a black binder clip.

Mateo stroked the top page, then held the pages in both hands and turned to Evan. Mateo's hands trembled a bit as he did so.

"Read this. This might have the answers you're looking for."

Evan slid his backpack from his shoulder, put down his phone, and gently took the pages from Mateo. He felt a rush of vibrational energy flood his body.

"What is it?"

"Please read it. You will understand."

"Can I take them with me? I gotta get to practice. I'm performing tonight."

Mateo felt as if Evan were asking to take a piece of his body with him, but his only answer was, "Yes." It was the only answer possible.

Evan held out his hand to shake Mateo's.

"I'll come back tomorrow. Will you be here?"

Mateo smiled. "In the afternoon."

Evan carefully placed the pages in his backpack, zipped it, slipped it over his shoulder, and looked back at Mateo one more time.

"Thank you," he said.

"Just one thing I want you to remember as you read," Mateo said.

"What's that, man?"

"Once you see it, you cannot un-see it."

Evan nodded his head and darted out the church door.

Mateo stood in silence for a long time. He wondered how this was unfurling. He had spent so many years alone with what he saw. He felt as if his heart would burst.

He went back to his keyboard, sat up straight, and placed his fingers on the keys. But then his head fell to his hands, and he began to cry.

Chapter 4

Evan pushed the door open to his meager hotel room, threw his backpack on the bed, and gently placed his guitar in the corner. He was pleased with his performance at Trinity Hall. In fact, he thought it might be his best one ever.

He smiled to himself, and then remembered the backpack. He spun around to the bed and gently straightened his pack before opening the zipper. He reached in and lifted the tattered pages. The cover page said, "The Nine Secrets to the Seer's Realm of the Kingdom."

Just then, he heard a gentle vibration from his guitar strings. He was filled with fear. His heart pounded in his chest. But then he remembered what Mateo had said. "Once you see it, you cannot un-see it."

He brushed his fear away, slumped in a seat in the corner with the lamp, and began to read.

Chapter Five

SECRET ONE: YOU CAN ACCESS THE SECRETS TO THE SEER'S REALM OF THE KINGDOM

"The seer's realm brings simplicity of focus."

—*Dr. Showalter Johnson*

In your hands you hold the instructions that will show you how to shift your life from one of existence to one of mastery. These words contain the secrets to the seer's realm of the Kingdom. It is a method to see beyond the earthly and every day, and guides you to find a way of viewing your life as a connected whole and to feel integrated with that whole: to achieve a sense of spirit.

But you must follow the protocols.

If you do you would become like the mustard seed. When it is planted, the mustard seed is very small, but it then grows to about six feet tall. It provides a place for the beast of the field to shelter and a feast for the birds in the tree. The roots, seeds, cabbage . . . all of it nourishes the strawberries, and they feed the rabbit. Then the wind blows, and the seeds grow elsewhere in the distance . . . and the mustard seed spreads abundance once again.

In the mustard seed is a village. When you download the image of the mustard seed, then you can really see what it is. The growth of a mustard seed is there for you. The mustard seed and its abundance change the surroundings and everything it reaches. It nourishes and nurtures and covers. The mustard seed shows you what you can do.

And how will you accomplish this feat?

The answer is simple. You begin with the end in mind.

In order to enter the seer's realm of the Kingdom, you must re-train your eyes to see. Every image in the Bible can be used to see what He wants for you and what He has for you to do.

Einstein said, "The last thing I do before I lay me down to sleep is ask my creator to give me something creative to think about Him." We have been *taught* information from the earthly world and how to retain it, but we need to *instill* information from the Kingdom world and how to retain it as well. Einstein showed us a way.

Every 15 minutes before going to bed, give your creator something meaningful to speak back to you. Study and cherish the rich Godly images available to you. Seek the meanings of those images. And then you will begin to learn.

Your dreams are where the divine reaches down to touch the everyday world. As you look at the rich images available to you, they will seep into your other mind and ignite your heart. Your dreams are where you can concentrate your intentions and desires for your spiritual growth.

As you sleep, you learn through your heart. Everything is pressed and processed through your heart, then it extends to your brain. Your inner man vibrates. Your body is a transmitter, and you learn through vibration. You begin to experience the magic and mystical capacity to see the Kingdom realm. Because the realm is not of this world but of the outer world, it means it cannot *give* you what you need on the inside to access this realm. You must see it. You must seek it. By training yourself to see, it gives the creator something to work with while you sleep. The Word of God is a trigger to open your inner eye.

Follow the secrets in these pages, and you will know what to do. Many books have been written and many sermons have been preached about the Kingdom. But have you ever asked the authors and the church leaders, "How do I access the Kingdom? What steps do I follow? How do I get to this higher level? How do I get to the seer's realm of the Kingdom?" Did you receive the answers?

Probably not. But you most likely heard them speak of hearing the voice of God and speak about reading the scriptures, but they've unlikely talked about what it is you need to do to see God. To see his Kingdom.

The answer is in the scriptures. "I will seek first the king." "I will seek His face."

It doesn't get any clearer than that.

Everyone has a birthright that is connected to God's face. When a seer is able to look into the face of God and see the four dimensions, they begin to understand they could never be a copy of the original, but are indeed made in the image and likeness of God. The four dimensions of His face can touch all people. The face is a mirror.

Ezekial explains the four pictures in God's face, and those are the eagle, the ox, the lion, and the human. Those four creatures represent the four dimensions of God's face. Ezekial said when I see His face I am disengaging from one Kingdom that is of the earth and coming into His Kingdom. The seer is having a relationship with the face of God.

His face gives you the privilege of holy ones to see the holy angels. When you see God's face you are corresponding with him. You are building a relationship with Him. His eyes contain the eyes to see how *He* sees.

The face of God is a mirror and reflection of all personalities and traits in the earthly realm. By learning these secrets, you can develop your seer's ability.

If you seek his face, He hears from heaven and then it is passed to you. It is not the other way around.

This prophetic anointing with the seer and the face gives the seer the ability to bring life to people who think that they have lost their identity. Each of us has an identity in the face of God. You carry it with you.

What is the meaning for the seer and his face? It is about helping people understand who they are. We carry dimensions of his face. Knowing that helps us to bring life to who we are . . . so our identity rests in God's Kingdom. The Kingdom is not about what you do, it's about who you are.

If we don't seek, He don't speak. It is your responsibility to first engage the Kingdom realm by seeing.

And how do you do this? Through these secrets it can be done, for each secret contains the protocols and the imagery to bring you closer to the Kingdom of God and ultimately the Kingdom of Heaven.

The inner journey is a quest for understanding and insight. Regardless of how much is known or learned, no information can be of true benefit until we have understood how to make the best use of it. This ability is defined as seeing. It is an alignment of thought, feeling, and body. Acquiring this ability is only available in the light of God's face.

To become a master in the ways of the seer, you must learn and practice the protocols of each secret in the right order. When you have followed the protocols accordingly, you can see all that is needed to align with the Kingdom of all that is.

Read them or do them in the wrong order, and you will see nothing. For all the glory that waits for you, turn your gaze toward it.

Chapter Six

SECRET TWO: GOD'S KINGDOM IS A GOVERNMENT

"We have been chosen for something greater than war. We have been chosen to open the eyes of all the nations, so that they can finally see that the Kingdom never failed."

—*Dr. Showalter Johnson*

The Kingdom is a government

Each of us has a kingly call for our lives. That kingly call is a role in God's government that He has selected you for. It's up to you to pick up the responsibility as well as the opportunity and live life to your fullest potential on earth.

God rules the government and we manage it

It is a government in which power is vested in the people by God. Therefore, that power is exercised by the people—whether directly or indirectly—through a *system* based on Biblical truths revealed by the Holy Spirit to each individual for the good of the Kingdom. The Word of God gives us many examples of the kingly and priestly anointing that's in the lives of many of the prophets and parables in the Bible. We'll examine many of them within the Secrets you now hold in your hands.

God's Kingdom is comprised of three courts

God's Kingdom has three courts, and you must engage with each one in the proper order before you can graduate to the next.

1. The Kingdom of Earth is the atmospheric presence of God. In order to access the Kingdom of Earth we must be able to *feel*. In the Kingdom of Earth we learn by vibration.

2. The Kingdom of God is the government inside of you where you manifest the 12 laws of the inner man. Kingdom of God is what we *profess*. It is God's rule. In order to access the Kingdom of God inside of you, you need to develop your ability to *see*.

3. The Kingdom of Heaven is God's domain outside of us. The Kingdom of Heaven is what you *possess*. It is where we have impact on our surroundings and on nations. It functions like a marketplace, and we must enter the marketplace on earth with our kingly anointing . . . that is, our role of government. And in our role, we are seated at the right hand of God that is nurturing and comforting and disciplining you. The hand shows a full provision. That's why scripture says the Kingdom of Heaven is *at hand*.

There are no class distinctions or privileges

God's Kingdom is not encumbered by a person's heredity or other arbitrary class distinctions or privileges. You are part of the Kingdom and the governments and the societies that are powered by free and creative-thinking people who believe in and practice the idea that all people are socially equal and God-endowed to become productive and fulfill their potential to advance His Kingdom.

When you look at a picture of a king, he is someone who acts in an administrative way. Take a look at Daniel, for instance, and the kingly aspect of Daniel's life. Daniel was a king as a part of his duty in the governmental realm. He was a politician and a governor . . . that was the kingly call on his life. That kingly call put him at the top of the spheres of influence. Your kingly call can do the same for you.

You have a sphere of influence

When you are seated in high places at the right hand of the Father, then you are in your sphere of influence. You are in your seat of authority. It is the *right* place for you to be. In that way, you are a co-laborer with Him. You are partners with Him. You are in relationship with Him. It is your calling.

Each of us is a king in God's government

His Kingdom is in me and it is in you. And we are ambassadors of government spheres with different roles and functions. There is something for everyone. It is a responsibility we must pick up and take on in our lives. It is a responsibility in which we can renew ourselves, our families, our friends, our neighbors, and ultimately, the world.

It is unfortunate that most people today are not in their seat of authority. They have not picked up their sphere of responsibility because they want God to do it for them, or they just don't know what it is. But what is our responsibility of being kings that we are kings of and how do we embody the words of God's Kingdom? What is our relationship with God in us?

This book can help you find out.

Modern lifestyles leave us little time to stop and consider the effect we have or are supposed to have in God's Kingdom. It is my hope that by understanding the components of the Kingdom, it will help you find your seat of authority by following the secrets in the pages that follow. Your life will never be the same if you do.

Chapter Seven

SECRET THREE: UNDERSTANDING JEWISH CULTURE HELPS YOU TO SEE

"When you engage in the seer's realm, you are measured by the refraction of the color index of your life."

—*Dr. Showalter Johnson*

Jewish culture is rich with parables, precepts, and protocols that help us to understand the seer's realm of the Kingdom. Study their culture, and it will explain the mysteries of returning God's government to earth.

Know the language

When you study the language of Jesus, you will find that His language birthed a rural culture. Every culture has a language. Jesus was a Jew and his language was Hebrew, but there was still a dialect that Jesus spoke . . . and it was Aramaic. Even though Aramaic and Hebrew may be the same language, their differences must be given attention in order to understand what Jesus was saying. Some of the words are the same, some are used interchangeably when they shouldn't be, and some are different altogether because of the dialects.

That is still true today. For example, in Spain, the citizens speak Spanish and there is a certain culture that is connected to their language. If you want to understand Spaniards, you not only have to understand their language but also their slang (or dialect). That's how their culture comes into play.

Cubans speak Spanish, too, but there are different meanings to the words Cubans use because they are from another part of the world . . . another culture. Mexicans speak Spanish too, but again . . . their cultural meanings of words are not the same as Cubans or Spaniards. Italians share many of the same words with Cubans, but with different spellings and different meanings.

So, in the same way that modern languages are the *same,* their cultures elicit *different meanings* of the words used. It's the same thing with Hebrew letters and Aramaic letters . . . they are similar, but not the same. This is an important distinction to remember when studying the language of Jesus. That is how you can tap into the rural culture that Jesus was birthed out of.

Read from the back of the book to the front

When the Jewish people read, they start at the back of the book and move to the front. When you read from the back of the book, you're starting from the right; and when you read to the front of the book, you're ending on the left. When you start from the right, that's where your creativity begins; and when you move to the left, that's where your logic begins. By reading this way, you will see things in a different way because your creativity is being activated first. You feel it differently.

When people began to read from left to right instead, we lost the proper direction of feeling and then sensing and then seeing. Because we have shifted the direction of how we read, we have shifted how we feel. But scriptures say, "Spirit moves the face of the water." That's vibration right there. By feeling the vibration, we learn. And then we see the light.

Because of this shift in direction, both literally and figuratively, what has happened is that our ability to decree and declare things over our life is met with major turmoil and confusion . . . simply because we are going the wrong way.

Before Satan fell from the heavens, the north used to be the south. When he fell, there was a shifting of the north and the south from a spiritual standpoint. If you think about that in the natural world, let's say you are in Florida and Miami is in the south and Jacksonville is in the north. What if the next time you came back to Florida, Miami was in the north and Jacksonville was in the south? Wouldn't you need a GPS? Yes, because you'd be lost.

God's Prophetic System (GPS) is a system to help people find direction in their lives by using this sacred tool. Go the right way by feeling first (that is, being creative first), and then you're able to pronounce and decree and declare things over your life more strategically and carefully. Just like your own personal GPS system.

But if you go the wrong way, if you do it the other way around, it is easy to see how confusion sets in. That is because that is not the culture of the Jews, and the Kingdom, and how we are intended to read. Think of a GPS that leads you the wrong way or to a dead end. You are met with confusion . . . and probably a lot of frustration.

Seeing trumps hearing

Jews were interested in doing what the Father does. The Greeks were more interested in doing what the Father says.

When you look at those two things, doing what the Father does versus doing what the Father says, you can see there's a better quality of understanding through seeing rather than hearing. If you are a father who has a son, and your son does as you do, it means your son must see you do it. You are his role model . . . his living example. Jesus said, "I only do what my Father does. Whatever I see my Father do, I do." He never said I do what my Father says.

Seeing is a higher quality than hearing. Unfortunately, there are many people who write books on hearing the voice of God, but hearing was never the first thing in the Jewish culture. It was always to see something.

Throughout the scriptures, most people saw things. And most things that happened in Israel were happening by a sign, and people had to see that sign in something they were seeing naturally. That sign was something spiritual. This corrects the major false principle of people wanting to learn how to hear the voice of God.

When you do as your Father does, then you are a seer. I saw my Father, who is of course Jesus, do what He did. So, I will do the same.

The 12 Colors of the Jewish Months

The 12 colors are very important to seers. In the seer's realm, we understand that there are 12 colors on the priest Ephod. Each color is connected to a Hebrew month. For example, the color red on the priest Ephod was connected to the month Nissan, which means April in Hebrew.

The Bible also speaks about the Joseph coat of many colors. This expresses the importance of the ability to see colors and to have an understanding, the wisdom, and the knowledge of what is really going on.

The month you were born in represents what I like to call "the color index of your life."

There are times when I'd see colors when speaking with someone that most of the time the color is connected with their birth date, or the color sometimes indicated a special month letting me know that something specific would happen in that month for a person. The month attached to the color is giving me a revelation of some miracle that is connected with that particular month from ancient Jewish times.

Months are marked with miracles

The 12 months do not only have 12 colors attached to them, but those 12 months are marked with prophetic events, and miracles have been repeating themselves over and over. The number 12 is so important because it's a number of government that helps to understand times and seasons.

When you study the event that took place at Mount Sinai, you discover there was a major miracle that took place on that date and time; therefore, this month has a sacred marking on it, and we continue to relive these miracles in some form on the same month date.

He who has the experience of moving in this dimension of the seers, not only see in color, but know the right months that connect with color. The meaning becomes a matter of time now that the months are involved.

The seers must understand time . . . not by managing the time, but by mastering the time.

One of the first things that seers and prophets understood was time and the Jewish calendar. The most important challenge to seers is not the ability to see, but the ability to see and master time by understanding how Jewish months connect with colors.

This is just one example how colors are used in the seer's realm. Remember, color receives its energy from light, and color animates worlds in the seer's dimension.

The angel Chameleon

Being able to see the 12 colors is being able to see the angelic being . . . an angel called Chameleon.

In Jewish studies, Chameleon comes when the presence of God is around and is in a place. There are two things to understand when

Chameleon comes. One time is when you go to God's domain, and the next time is when He comes to you.

Examine Jewish trading practices

Jewish people practice collaborative trading. They had their banking system, and they kept it in their own circle. In other words, they traded among themselves . . . their monies, their trade, and their circle. And that's why you see so many of the Jewish people wealthy today. They still have that inequality that makes them distinctive as a people because they lend monies within their own culture. They have their own community and ways of doing things, and that is their trading secret. The manner in which they traded monies and relied on merchants and purchased different products created a collaborative matrix for them to do business and to empower their own people.

Constantine demanded to know how the Jews received all this money. Once he found out, he broke it up. Constantine destroyed the circle and took the monies from them. Because of this, that trading quality of collaboration was lost, and the church no longer has it.

The structure of the courts

Jewish people set up the structure of the courts composed of three judges responsible for the matters of religious law and settlement of civil disputes in three areas . . . marriage, divorce, and inheritance. The Beth Din were three wise men over the court system and coordinated with the synagogue. (Today it is separated, which is a dichotomy.) They knew how to legislate the 12 judicial Laws of Jerusalem and could discern which of the 12 laws was connected to a court case. The Beth Din who presided over the church is important because it mirrors that which is in heaven.

The importance of the pattern of three

The number three is important because it means to be caught up in the heavenly supply. It is also the protocol as set by the Jewish court system. By interpreting God's government correctly, we will be able to re-establish it on earth.

Let's look at Zechariah. In Zechariah 3:7, it says I will allow you to judge my house. When Zechariah makes that proclamation, he is also saying the house of covenant that I'm entering into is a house that you want me to judge. Elijah is the prophet who used the principles of Zechariah on Mount Carmel when he was dealing with the prophets of Baal and dealing with the Jezebel spirit. He stood up against 450 false prophets. And when he did, he made the declaration to make a statement to the Lord of Abraham, Isaac, and Jacob. In other words, he was saying don't let me be embarrassed in front of all these people. I represent your Kingdom. I'm coming against these false prophets. I need the Lord of Abraham, Isaac, and Jacob to stand up for me.

This is an example in the scriptures that you can use to practice in your prayer life and in life. When Elijah says, Lord of Abraham, Isaac, and Jacob, I need you to stand up for me, *he is telling the seer what to see when they read that.* They should see when they read that statement (Abraham, Isaac, and Jacob) that Elijah is entering the house of covenant and you would allow me to judge your house. Elijah is judging the house of Israel. When Elijah mentions Abraham, Isaac, and Jacob, he is operating as the Beth Din by mentioning those three, and he's judging over the nation of Israel.

When Elijah made that declaration that he was entering into the house of covenant through the pathway to multiply, God responds with fire. For the seer, when God responds back by fire, God is saying I want to multiply Elijah, the covenant of my Kingdom, so that I can look at it and bestow my power in it.

You can practice this theme. This is why it's called "The Seer's Beth Din." It is the ability to see the Kingdom, the ability to see it through the bench of three, and through the patterns of three in scripture. And it's saying God wants you to multiply the covenant of His government so that He can look at it and bestow and restore His power in it.

The Beth Din

What is this bench of three, the Beth Din?

When we look at it through the Hebrew language, it is important to look at the old pictorial Hebrew language. Every letter had a picture, so it provides a better understanding of what the Jews really meant. With the new Hebrew language, you're not able to see into that realm of what that world really means.

If you look at the word BETH in the pictorial language, it is the picture of a house. And it shows someone going into a house (or the power of covenant).

Looking at it further, it says then we go to the DIN, which is a picture of a door. Something moving into multiplication. So, this is another example of when you take the word Beth Din all together, it's really saying it is entering into the house of covenant through the pathway to multiply.

Unraveling this is an aspect of teaching people how to see into God's Kingdom from the scriptures.

When we look in the scriptures how do we see this? How do we see the Beth Din in the Word of God? How do we take this and look at the scripture and practice it? Well, let's examine it more closely.

When Elijah said the Lord God of Abraham, Isaac, and Jacob . . . that's the bench of three in that scripture. As we've discovered from Jewish culture, that bench of three is actually a protocol system of God's Kingdom. God wants to lay a foundation of his Kingdom upon those declarations from the prophet. Because that's the shadow of heaven. That's the protocol system. So, when Elijah says the Lord of Abraham, Isaac, and Jacob, it is important to remember that Abraham to the Jewish people is God. Isaac to the Jewish people is Jesus. And Jacob to the Jewish people is the Holy Spirit. So, Elijah is really saying, "God the Father, God the Son, God the Holy Spirit." Abraham, Isaac, and Jacob.

So that's the Beth Din. That's the three. That's the pattern. That's the protocol system and the foundation of heaven is being laid upon that through his proclamation.

You can understand and practice this by finding scripture that has things in patterns of threes. That's how you'll know this is the Beth Din. This is how seers use the Beth Din in scripture . . . those things that are coming in patterns of threes. They begin to see into the Kingdom realm and know that God is speaking and wanting to lay a foundation. And through that, God wants to enter them into a house of covenant and take them into a pathway to multiply.

The number three is like a governmental protocol. Wherever you see three, or the number three, or three things happening, or three names being mentioned in a pattern, or in the tabernacle (outer court, inner court, holiest of holies), you are reading about protocols.

In the courts of the tabernacle, the outer court was accessible, but then it was a protocol to move to the second inner court, and then there was another protocol to move to the third. Because you didn't walk in on the King just like that. Just like if there are protocols in governmental agencies to meet the President, there's a certain protocol that you would have to follow in order to meet that President. You just don't walk in on him.

In the first 70 years of the church, every church had a bench of three before Constantine took over and changed it. Because the bench of three is also a picture of the trinity, three in one.

It is also a shadow whenever you see the pattern of threes where God wants to lay His Kingdom government on His foundation of His Kingdom on the bench of three. And that meant He will come up on us. When that bench of three is re-established as a structure on Earth, then God looks for a structure that looks like Himself and comes upon us.

In the scripture, the Bible says around the throne of God is the Godhead. The Godhead is the trinity. It's God the Father, God the Son, and God the Holy Spirit that's around the throne. The Beth Din. The three again is around God's throne. So, God is saying if I can get that stuff established in the Earth, then the Kingdom of Heaven sees something that looks like itself, and then it comes upon them, and then it begins to multiply them.

The cognitive picture of Beth Din was three wise men who presided over the church. That three is important because it mirrors an image in heaven (the images of the Godhead in heaven that sits on the throne is three in one), and the Beth Din on earth mirrors that which is in heaven.

Chapter Eight

SECRET FOUR: FOLLOW THE PROTOCOLS

"The future holds something that the past never had."

—Dr. Showalter Johnson

In order to go to Him, it requires a protocol. It's a divine order that you follow so that you can engage and access the seer's realm of the Kingdom. These are the protocols to see in God's government. The protocols are accessed by faith and not by what you see in the natural, but by what you see in the spiritual.

I am teaching the protocols on how you move from engaging with the presence of God and how to be host for the Kingdom of God within. Then moving into the Kingdom of Heaven which is the domain outside of us, and how to get that to come over us. Let's now learn the protocols for how to move into that.

Protocol One: Follow the Divine Order of the Kingdom

"Divine order unleashes divine flow."

The divine order is this: First the Kingdom of Earth. Move to the next level which is Kingdom of God. Move to the next level which is the Kingdom of Heaven

And by following the protocols is how you will achieve it.

Protocol Two: Fast

"Fasting allows the heart to go were the mind can't go."

Whenever we enter a new year, I place prophets and seers on the Elijah's fast. Fasting is necessary to cleanse and heal the past, so you can see. When you fast, just like Elijah, it's to get you right first. We can see this in the scripture about Elijah's fast. Fasting is necessary because when you attempt to go to a new level in the Kingdom, you will be attacked by a lot of things in your soul from your past that want to prevent you from seeing. So, the Elijah fast is needed as a protocol to help facilitate the faculty of the inner eye, the inner man.

The purpose of Elijah's fast is to speed up your ability to feel and see and slow down your ability to think (which is your flesh). Because when you are moving in the realm of the spirit, there's no time to think. So, your ability to see is now heightened. Discernment is a way of seeing as well. The importance of Elijah's fast is so you can discern and appraise what God is showing you to do.

The soul is a mirror

The soul, body, and spirit are like the Beth Din of our lives. Once all three are in alignment, your Beth Din can mirror and project the correct images in your head while empowering you with clarity and direction. Elijah's soul was out of alignment; therefore, the bench of three in his life (the soul, body, and spirit) was not as one, which is the reason he saw unclearly and developed feelings of suicide. Elijah's fast helped to restore the Beth Din of Elijah's life. It can do the same for you.

Protocol Three: Know the order for engaging in the Kingdom

5. Touching . . . points what you speak by faith into the direction.
4. Speaking . . . what you speak are words, and words have values attached to them. What you speak are words which,

metaphorically, serve as wood and material to create your world.

3. Smelling . . . when we smell it's like a fragrance. Smell also represents vibration, so knowledge is like fragrance.

2. Hearing . . . enables our ability to respond. People remember about 20 percent of what they hear.

1. Seeing . . . the highest level of engaging the Kingdom. Starts within and are pure, nonverbal thoughts.

Protocol Four: Feel

It's interesting to note that all Hebrew letters are connected to the word "yud" which means hand. Every letter that has a value connected with it has a design, and all things spoken have the hand involved . . . we create with our hands, we express with our hands, and our hands point the direction for us.

This explains the importance of feeling and making sure we know how to feel.

Based on what you speak, you are pointing to your passion and purpose in the direction that will help you to frame your world.

Protocol Five: Seek His Face

"The beauty of a face is the harmony of its parts."

The face of God is a reflection and mirror of all the different personalities and traits. Learning the dimensions of God's face is all about developing your seer's ability.

The face is broken up into four parts

There is a teaching about the Moses tabernacle. A tabernacle is where his presence dwells with humankind, and we have already studied how the face of God dwells with all humankind as it relates to all of the tribes of Israel.

But in this case, the face of God is dwelling in the tabernacle of Moses, and it is concealed. You can reveal the face of God that is hiding in the tabernacle by using instruments that connect with the function of a face.

1. The Holiest of Holies was at the top. This was considered the head of God. There was a box, and in the box were the two tablets of stones . . . which was the law. The box is the head, and, in the box, you have the tables that represent the brain's "cognitive abilities."

2. Just under the ark you have the two eyes. Positioned on the left you had the seven candle sticks (which would be the left eye), and on the right side would be the table with "showbread" adjacent to it. The concept is that the seven candlesticks provide the light (the left eye) in order to show the showbread (the right eye).

3. Just under the eyes you have the sense Alta, which relates to smell, and that relates to the noise. The golden Sensor was used to sense a smell and that is the function of the noise, so we call it the nose.

4. Just below we have this long thing that looks like a mouth, it's an Alta where things are consumed, it's called the brazen Alta. Of course, we consume things with the mouth.

It's clear that the strategic positioning of all of those instruments in the tabernacle were positioned in the same place of a face, and they all possess the functions of the different parts of the face. They all line up with the corresponding function of a face, but what does this mean?

Upon the completion of the tabernacle, there was a priestly blessing that was pronounced by Aron the high priest, and his sons would say:

Let God bless you and keep you, let God shine his face upon you, and grant you grace, let God lift up his face to you and grant you peace.

What word keeps on appearing there? Face. It means that God turns toward us, favors us, and grants us things . . . like peace.

Leviticus 9:22 is the first blessing that was mentioned by Aron after the building of the tabernacle, because the face of God was concealed in the tabernacle.

Four creatures represent four dimensions of God's face

There are 12 Hebrew months, and everyone has a Jewish month. Moses separated tribes into four sets of three . . . three in the east, three in the south, three in the west, and three in the north.

1. The lion—east and the three months of April, May, and June.
2. The human—south and the three months of July, August, and September.
3. The ox—west and the three months of October, November, and December.
4. The eagle—north and the three months of January, February, and March.

Every month is connected to a tribe.

Each month has a personality trait that can be seen in the face of anyone connected to a certain month.

Judah (April): This person is a leader.

Issachar (May): This person is the scholar.

Zebulun (June): This person is the business person.

Reuben (July): The first born, unstable like water. The person in this month brings life, but if you neglect them, if you don't channel or guide them, they can get out of control.

Simeon (August): This person is aggressive. They can have a cruel wrath against their enemies, but their aggressiveness can be used for the good.

Gad (September): This person is a warrior.

Ephraim (October): This person represents transformation.

Manasseh (November): This person represents reconnection.

Benjamin (December): This person is a ravenous consumer.

Dan (January): This person is a judge.

Asher (February): This person is the prosperous one.

Naphtali (March): This person is a free spirit.

"The Kingdom is not about what you do, but who you are."

Remember, everyone with a certain birth date will find that there is a prophetic dimension corresponding with the face of God that is connected to them through their birth. When you begin to understand it, God begins to show you things about who you are.

Protocol Six: Know the two most important agents of sin—the heart and the eyes

When engaging the Kingdom, you must know how to use these two agents. The eyes represent the world without and the heart represents the world within.

1. *See* **with your heart first.** The heart is full of seeds. Whatever you see causes those seeds to germinate and develop into desires.
2. **Do not *hear* with your heart first.** If you hear with your heart first, you might not get the message. He is not always coming in the sound of thunder and lightning, but in the still, small voice.

   Many people hear with their hearts first and become vulnerable to voices that may not be the voice of God, hence they experience major confusion.

Protocol Seven: Seeing is a higher quality than hearing

When a seer sees something, they see from the end, which is the right brain, which is our creative capacity. Then hearing starts from the left brain, which is the logical aspect. When we seek God's Kingdom, we have to recognize that. If you try to hear before you see, then you're going to be in confusion. You're going to hear voices of your ego. You're going to hear false voices. But if you learn how to see first, which is the end, then you can download images on the inside of you. Then you can begin to *respond* in faith by what you *see.*

Protocol Eight: Whatever you look at in life, you get changed into

That's another reason why seeing spiritually (not in the natural) is more important than hearing. There are scriptures in the Bible, of course, and images that we can use to trigger our Godly imagination. Practicing that and being able to see in the spiritual realm, seeing in God's Kingdom, and seeing first is far more powerful and valuable than hearing first.

Protocol Nine: Use hearing to respond

If you are trying to hear the voice of something that's in the spiritual world or someone who you haven't seen, it means that the quality is not going to be very clear.

Most of the prophets in the Bible, like Ezekiel, say they were lifted up. When Ezekiel was lifted up, the Lord asked him what he saw. He saw a Kingdom, and that's what it is. It's not what he heard. The only time he said that, he said, "Faith comes by hearing." And that's a response, a response to something. He was lifted up, and the Lord showed him, showed him a Kingdom.

John also was lifted up, and he saw Jerusalem. Most of the things that happened, these prophets or seers saw first in the realm of the spirit. Then they were able to hear the voice of God after. It was not hearing the voice of God first, before they had intimacy with God, because what that does is that defies the protocol.

Responding in faith is based on our obedience to God. You cannot respond in faith and be obedient if you don't know him. A lot of people are being told to have faith, and they're trying to respond in obedience, but they don't have the downloads. They don't have the protocol. They haven't engaged the presence. They haven't been able to understand that before they can really do some things as a protocol, they must engage their presence. Then they enter into the Kingdom of God, which is the domain inside. The next realm is the Kingdom of Heaven, which is the domain outside. There are protocols, so trying to have faith without going through the right protocol makes our faith confused.

Paul says in the book of Romans that there are many voices in the earth, and those voices in the earth when we respond to them create an atmosphere and sustain it. Most people have trouble trying to hear the voice of God because they haven't seen Him first.

For example, the scripture says seek first the Kingdom and then there's another scripture that faith comes only by hearing. It doesn't come by seeing. Because in order for you to have faith, you have to see something first. When you look at the divine protocol of the Kingdom, the first thing to do is seek and the word s-e-e is in seek. As you seek, you begin to see God's Kingdom. You begin to enter into His realm. When you see God's Kingdom that is in you, then now whatever you have seen in you, you can respond to it by faith.

Unfortunately, what people are doing is shifting it in the other direction. They're trying to have faith, but they have never seen the domain that they host of God's Kingdom on the inside of them, so they have no understanding. Instead you must see the realm of the Kingdom and host it on the inside of you, and *then* faith comes by hearing. Now whatever you hear, your faith is a response based on what you see. That's what hearing the voice of God is for, but the body of Christ shifted it around. They're trying to hear God's voice first, but they haven't seen him. They haven't seen His Kingdom, and He gave a divine order.

Protocol Ten: Animate your dreams with your soul

The soul is your Pixar that gives you the ability to animate characters. And you can feel through those characters. That's how powerful the soul is. Our soul is between the gate of Earth and Heaven. And when we have dreams, our soul is animating the dreams. And there are some dreams that are so lucid, there are some dreams that we can actually feel because we are Pixaring our own world through our soul. We are creating characters through our soul that we can feel.

Protocol Eleven: Stand in your governmental protocol

The Kingdom cannot be given to adolescents. If we are out of protocol, that means we are not standing in our governmental protocol. So, we never grow up to be kings. We stay sons and daughters. We remain adolescents.

What that is really speaking about is many people can see things. They can give a prophetic word, but a lot of their energies are undeveloped.

Protocol Twelve: Engage the presence of God

You have to engage the presence of God. Engaging the presence of God is all about intimacy. You get to see him. You get to know him by seeing him. You get to see him do things. You get to understand more about his Kingdom realm.

If you haven't engaged God's presence so you can have an intimacy with Him and learn about Him first, then you don't graduate to the Kingdom of God and learn how to be a good host of His domain on the inside of you. If you don't know how to be a host of the Kingdom of God, then you never graduate into understanding how to deal with the Kingdom of Heaven.

Protocol Thirteen: Train your inside man about truth

When you do that, what's inside of you is connected to two thirds of your brain. We have to be seers, and we have to be able to see from on the inside, which is a different way of behaving.

Protocol Fourteen: Train your inner man to see impressions around you

We have to begin to train our inner man to see impressions around us. Remember, we learn by vibrations and our bodies attract, literally, like an antenna. This will help you overcome the outside man from the inside. The things around us begin to control what we see on the inside of us. But when we use the Word of God and allow the images there, we can overcome the outside man from the inside.

Protocol Fifteen: Vision has a progression to be followed

1. Looking. It is intentional (like looking at a newspaper). You can also look for insight into something.
2. Watching. It is watching something move (like watching a movie). It is a strategic positioning where time is involved. You are watching patterns.
3. Seeing is the highest level of anointing. It is the ability to see in the spiritual realm, the Kingdom realm, the eternal realm. You see images no matter what you do.

Protocol Sixteen: The future is behind you; the past is in front of you

The future for most people is something in front of them, and the past is in the back of them. That is a major confusion because the future, according to the Jews, is actually behind you, and the past is actually in front of you. When we look at the word past, the past is always like "re." The word "re" is restoring, reforming. "Re" is going back to its original intent.

Now, think about it. When a person says they are stuck in their past, what do they do? They continue to go back to the thing in their mind, back to the hurt, back to the pain, and back to all that doesn't serve them. They "re"turn back to the original intent of something, whether the intent is good or bad. When you live in the past, you go back to that. When you place the past in the back of you, it is confusion because it has no place to go. "Re" is almost like in a circle.

It takes you back to where you started. Let's say you got in your car, you left home, you drive around the bend, and you're back home. You went nowhere.

When you place the past in front of you and the future behind you, this is how it really looks. The future really starts in your mind. It really starts in your brain, and that's where we see things. That's where we paint things. That's how to move and break free from the toxic stuff of your past.

But if you follow the straight line of time, you stay in the wrong time and space. If the past is always behind you, it is the wrong strategic positioning, which is why you always keep it. You always condemn yourself with it. It becomes a shadow that's over your reputation and over your life. And then people can see that shadow, and you know the importance of shadows. That negativity of your past, once it's a shadow behind you, it always looks for itself and so it will always stay over you.

Remove the shadow from behind you. Put it in front of you so you can hold it accountable, and it will take you back to a new season in your life to begin with God.

Protocol Seventeen: Use two thirds of your brain to control the other third, not the other way around

When you move or read or learn from left brain to right brain, you only access one third of your brain. That means you are allowing the potential of a lot of things to go unused.

If you think, "God is going to do something," that is left brain, right brain. That's not the right order. But if you're perceiving the future to be behind and the past in front, when you see things, you see them in a whole different direction. You're going to say, "God already did it." When you say, "God already did it," then you see whatever has been bound on earth has already been bound in heaven. That is in his past, perfect, future tense. That's how seers of the Kingdom see: past, perfect, future tense.

In the Book of Matthew, Chapter 16, when it says, "Whatever you bind on earth shall be bound in heaven," that is incorrect. That "shall be bound" is actually pronouncing confusion because that's not the original. When you say whatever has been bound on earth has already been bound, that means in your mind, "Okay, the future is actually behind me and the past is in the front of me, and then God is taking me back to do something new in my life, so I can continue to grow." That is the dynamic of seeing things from the back of the book to the front. The dynamics of seeing the future behind us instead of front of us. The dynamics of vision. We're starting from the end so that our planning can start from the beginning, and then continue to move on.

Unfortunately, most people today are only using one third of their brain. That's why they can't access the Kingdom of God from within because they can't see. When a person accesses only one third of their brain, there is another percentage that is left over. That percentage that remains leaves spaces, dark holes, other influences, and dark places in the brain.

There's a thin line between faith and fantasy, and that thin line with fantasy is that when we're only using one third of our brain, we allow different pockets to be opened for other things like witchcraft, fantasy, and false things to fill our mind. When we're moving with faith, we're actually using two thirds of our brain.

The danger of not using two thirds of your brain is leaving those empty pockets to be filled from the outside world. Other things like television, advertising, peer pressure, envy, and more. They fill those empty spaces in your brain.

The inner man is two thirds. The outer man is one third. When you go by, what you see outside is you using only one third of your brain. That is the conscious realm, and that is a smaller portal. When you use your inner man, when you understand the Kingdom of God that is in you, it has ability to teach you how to see God's realm in you that is not of this world. You depend on how to see from within and how to access two thirds of your brain, so everything can be covered. Everything can be used by God, so you can see what He wants for you and what He has for you.

Protocol Eighteen: Be a good host

Once we have been a good host for the domain of God's Kingdom inside of us, then we pass the test. Then we begin to experience and tap into that atmosphere. Then we can move to the Kingdom of Heaven.

Chapter Nine

SECRET FIVE: USE YOUR IMAGINATION TO TRAIN YOURSELF TO SEE

"The vision is the end; the design and planning is the beginning."

—Dr. Showalter Johnson

You know what's so interesting in the Bible? There are many rich images that have been given to us to help us trigger our Godly imagination. That's what those images are there for. That is how they are to be used. We can use imageries in the Bible to show us how to see His Kingdom. The Bible uses imagery to trigger the eye of the inner man in the spiritual realm while we live in the earthly realm. So, the images are two-fold.

What we have done is given our minds over to other external images in the earthly realm (such as cars and movies and music lyrics and fashion and video games). We become detached, disenfranchised, and disillusioned from the Godly imagination and the world of the Kingdom that's on the inside of us. So that is all we see when we go to bed.

But what's beautiful about the design of God's Kingdom is that we are already downloaded with images about how to see. They are embedded inside of us. We just need to train ourselves to see them.

"Seeing is God's social strategy."

When we engage God's Kingdom by seeing within, the Kingdom provides a covering. His government covers our imagination and allows our eyes to see things pure and singular . . . unmixed. Without the Kingdom guiding and covering our eyes, we can end up seeing things that expose things that are not healthy for us. I call it seeing with fallen eyes.

We need to develop our visionary capacity

In order to develop the Kingdom of God within us, we must use the Bible to trigger our Godly imagination. Many have been taught to be afraid of our imaginations because we've been told that it is something demonic. I know there's a thin line between faith and fantasy, but we're not talking about fantasy. We're talking about Godly imagination and using the Word of God. Those images that are in the Book of Revelation are meant for us to use and to see.

Remember when we discussed the image of the mustard seed? The mustard seed is a Godly image.

If a person thinks about something long enough, he is going to go and do it. This is how you access it. The Kingdom of God is on the inside of us, and we are highly imaginative as Kingdom citizens. By using imagery in the Bible, we can begin to see from the world within, not from the world without.

A great way to picture this is by studying the story of Walt Disney and the creation of Disneyland.

"The greatest illusion to the eye is time."

When Disney looked out across large plot of land in Southern California, he saw images in his head. Mickey Mouse and Donald Duck. Goofy and Dumbo. Princes and Princesses. You name it. Then he imagined glorious buildings and a colorful setting for what was to become "The Happiest Place on Earth."

After seeing this vision in his mind, he hired artists to draw these images as well as architects and engineers to build what he saw. He had to hire all sorts of people to do a myriad of things . . . from plumbing to customer service to engineering spectacular rides. Disney didn't just have a thought of doing it. He was reliving what he envisioned in his mind. When he hired and brought together all the people to create, you might think that was the beginning of the process. But, they didn't just begin. They were reliving it with a blueprint.

When Disney saw what he saw stretching out across that vast piece of property, that's when the characters were created. He started to create these characters inside his head. He started to feel through these characters. The more he started to feel through these characters, the more he saw and the more Disneyland came to be. Think about it. Another person driving past that very same piece of land saw nothing. But after Disney saw the characters and what was possible, he began to feel through the characters. Then, the characters now had a sense of life on the inside of them that made them real.

The story of Walt Disney shows that the future behind us is like a first beginning "intention." When Disney's vision manifested in the natural, that's when the workers re-live the thoughts of the visionary.

Vision starts from the end

In the mind of the visionary, the future starts in the mind. The Bible says in Ecclesiastes that the end is better than the beginning. Disney saw everything at the end, and when the workers began, they started from the beginning . . . which was planning and design.

If I see the future in back of me and the past in front of me, then when I begin to decree things over my life, I do so without creating confusion. I see the future and the past in their strategic positions. If

I'm going to see things, it's not going to be what God is *going* to do . . . it is what God has *already done.*

Jesus set the stage so we could see

Jesus knew that man is on earth. We were created as spirit beings and made human after the fall after Adam and Eve picked from the tree. One of the parables that Jesus speaks about is one of the ways to get our inner man and woman to engage and see by dealing where God is and by where man is . . . that is, on earth.

When Jesus was healing people, what He was doing was catching the euphoria of supernatural. Kind of like Instagram does today. When people are catching pictures, they are sending images to others that they would not normally think about. Jesus used miracles as pictures to stage the Kingdom of God so that believers were able to *see* these miracles. Seeing was used as a social strategy to attract followers. And why was he staging it through miracles? Not for himself. He was staging it for God.

"Miracles stage the kingdom."

A leader creates a stage for others to perform on

John the revelator was a seer who saw in symbols. He saw pictures of heaven with angels, seven witnesses, the judge, and 24 elders. This is really a prophetic picture of the structure of a court system revealed in John's visions. Because we have these rich images that have been given to us, we can use them when engaging God's Kingdom. It shows us how things look; therefore, we can use these images as a blueprint that helps us engage the Kingdom of God.

We must train our inner man to see impressions around us

In order to help us overcome the outside man from the inside, remember to use the Word of God to allow the images there. The outside man, the things all around us, are beginning to control what we see on the inside of us. Remember to use the Bible to open up the retainable potential of our memory of the Kingdom . . . give it revelation with new information and an anchor to retain the two thirds of your brain.

Remember the genius of Einstein when he talked about asking his creator to give him something creative to think about before he laid down to go to sleep? You can do the same thing. Retain information from the spiritual realm before bed to open your inner man or woman. Ten minutes before you go to bed, engage in the spiritual and make sure the imagery you're watching is related to spiritual principles, rather than earthly ones. If we're going to be seers in the Kingdom realm, we have to see and learn how to retain what we see.

Your soul must be in alignment

If your soul is hosting your spirit, then your spirit is going to be the altar, and your soul is going to be the host. That's not the way we're designed. The soul in the tabernacle is always in the inner court. An inner sensor. Helps you to sense things.

Most people's souls are out of alignment due to major trauma (whether divorce, car accident, loss, grief, or pain). But your spirit/body/soul are supposed to be in alignment and integrated. That's where you get the word integrity. So, a person whose soul has experienced a trauma, those people may be healed in their body, but they haven't necessarily dealt with the trauma. In their soul is still fear.

I was visiting a friend in the hospital. She was healing in her body. But, as a seer, I told her that I saw her soul was still out of alignment with her body and spirit. I could still see scars in her soul. She didn't have anyone to talk to her soul, so she was not free.

I grabbed her ankles and pulled them. I was pulling her back into alignment. It is a picture of divine positioning. If there's no divine positioning, you won't get divine presence and power.

If your soul is out of alignment, you're out of divine position. No promise, no presence, no divine power.

Some have fallen eyes

There are many people who are seeing with fallen eyes and not Kingdom eyes. There are many seers who are not of the Kingdom. They are spiritual, yes, but their process is false under themselves because they are filled with words, and their pronunciation, and their phonics are filled with confusion. Because of that, they see with fallen eyes, meaning that when they're prophesying the future and the past in the wrong direction, when they don't see it correctly from within, that's how they see with fallen eyes and when their vision is mixed.

Blessed are the pure in hearts for they shall see God.

See there is singular.

Allow your sight to be singular

Seeing God is really seeing His Kingdom and really seeing the direction that we should be looking in. The future in front of us actually takes us into a dead end. When individuals see something new that is coming on the outside (such as a new car or a new smartphone), it gets them excited and wanting to have it. It's very manipulative and deceptive. People buy the new product. Then after a few months, it's not exciting anymore. If you want to stop seeing with fallen eyes want to see with Kingdom eyes, then allow your sight to be singular, allow it to be pure, and allow it to be on God's Kingdom, allow it to be all about his Kingdom.

"Seeing brings simplicity of focus."

See with Kingdom eyes

There's a movie about a martial artist, Bruce Lee, who fights while blindfolded. He had to be able to sense in order to fight. He has to sense and see what direction the person he is fighting is coming from. How is he sensing it? Not by thinking. This demonstrates the concept of seeing in the Kingdom. When it comes to faith, you cannot think. You have to vibrate. You have to sense, and you have to see it.

Bruce Lee was blindfolded, so he had to literally see from within himself and feel what's going on around him in order to be able to defeat his enemy. That seeing concept is the same feature of the strategy of how *we* see. Learning to see from the outside realm will give you fallen eyes. Learning to see from within will give you Kingdom eyes.

Open up your memory

Using the Word of God as a trigger will allow you to open up the retainable potential of your memory of the Kingdom and give it revelation, new information, and an anchor to retain the two-thirds part of your brain that has not been used before. That's so important. When there's an empty space, devils fill it. But when you have retained Godly images, there is no space to allow the devil to fill it.

WHAT STOPS US FROM SEEING?

There's a rich metaphoric picture again in the Old Testament that shows us what is really stopping people. The Bible says that God ripped the veil, but it was not just a veil that He ripped. It was not just the fabric. It was something more important.

It was the cherub on the veil. And this cherub was a messenger. It was an angel, and the angel was sewn into the fabric of the veil. That was the real mystery, and you had a lot of people saying, "Oh, God ripped the veil so we have access to Him," but they missed the main metaphoric picture there. It was that cherub that was sewn into the veil in the Book of Exodus, which was a metaphor for a type of fallen angel, that came to really veil them from really seeing into the Kingdom world. That same cherub, that same angel today, is *still* veiling people from being able to see into the Kingdom realm. That's important to recognize.

The first time the Bible spoke about seer's prophets in the Old Testament shows that a prophet is actually a communicator, but the seer is someone who just sees. Putting that in the proper perspective so that when you begin to see, you begin to understand God's realm of the Kingdom much more easily.

People fear engaging in the Kingdom world

They're afraid to go there. The spiritual world has presented to us voices that the devil is more powerful. Most of us see this today that the satanic world has been painted or shown to be more powerful, so it leaves us afraid as believers from accessing these realms.

We are afraid because we have been taught that using our imagination is unGodly, and fantasy is not of God. We've been taught in the church to stop imagining. The church tells us not to get into our imagination because it's demonic or the satanic world.

But the Bible clearly states that we were created in the image of God. Image is created to and connected to imagination. If we were created in the image of God, we have imagination of God in us. That's the Kingdom of God. We should access it.

We've allowed images to be blocked

Seeing images from the eternal realm means we see no matter what we do. We have been anointed with it . . . it's in us, no matter what we do we cannot stop it. That is a realm of seeing. Even though we have things within us that we can see from God's Kingdom, it is present, but it is not active.

For example, if you put batteries into a radio, but you don't place them strategically correct, then the radio will not function. They are present, but because they are not strategically correct they are not active. So, for many of us, we have visions to see no matter what. Nothing can stop us from seeing these God images and engaging in God's Kingdom. But for some reason, what happened to many of us, is we have been taught how to disengage from that ability to see.

Bad memories

There are certain imageries that we have seen that inform our memories and that we resist. These memories have resisted our spirit man from engaging memories of the Kingdom realm. These are memories from Sunday school or a lot of confusing things that we learned in the Bible when we were too young to understand.

We also may have many unrepentant memories that flicker in and out, and they work with the truth in dealing with our stuff. Then, we have a lot of demonic triggers as well connected into our spirit that we need to deal with that are preventing us from seeing . . . things from our past or familiar spirits. Remember, anything that comes from light is destroyed. When we begin to press into that seer's realm, we begin to destroy those things that hold us back.

Outside influences block images

Some people, if they haven't seen a chair, they can't see it. For example, I like to practice seeing things in the class with my students. I say to my students, "Close your eyes and imagine seeing the rain." There are people who could do it, but they struggled with it, and there were people who couldn't do it at all.

The Bible says, "I hear an abundance of rain." I was teaching about that, and everyone was jumping around and happy. I said, "Okay, close your eyes and I want you to see the abundance of rain." Nobody really could see it. One or two persons saw it after five minutes. They struggled. Why? Because the influence of what they see outside of themselves has dictated what they can see on the inside of themselves.

Now, if I ask them to see a BMW, or a Mercedes, or fashion designer clothing, they were able to see that very exactly. Why? Because they have been conditioned. Those material things have been conditioned in their heads to see those things, but when I said to show me rain and tell me if you see rain, they couldn't see that. I said, "Tell me if you can see a flaming sword?" They couldn't see that. "Tell me if you can see a man with gray long hair." They struggle to see that.

Most of the biblical images in the Bible are unable to be seen by most. You know why? They were able to see more outer things, worldly things like cars and stuff, and there's nothing wrong with what they were able to touch. These things are pictures and images that have more influence over their imagination, so those are the things that block people from really accessing and seeing into the Kingdom realm. They have not created the pictures in their head of Godly images so that they didn't have to see it to see it.

We were taught not to see

I was raised in the Catholic school. I'd see the blackboard, and when I'd close my eyes I'd see blackness. I was not engaging . . . like a tv screen that's off. Our imagination has been disengaged from the blackboards like the imagery of the cherub and the veil. When I close my eyes I cannot see, so we've learned how to be disengaged from seeing from those blackboards.

Chapter Ten

SECRET SIX: ENGAGE THE ATMOSPHERIC PRESENCE OF GOD IN THE KINGDOM OF EARTH

"Kings outrank princes."

—*Dr. Showalter Johnson*

The Kingdom of Earth was created in the Book of Genesis, chapter one, verse one. "In the beginning, God created the heavens and the earth." When the Lord separated Adam from Eve, this was the point where the atmospheric aspect of the earth was created. Again, Earth itself was created in Genesis, but Adam and Eve's separation created the atmospheric aspect of the Earth.

When we speak about the Kingdom of Earth, we're not speaking about the natural earth we walk on. We're speaking about the atmospheric aspect of the earth. When we deal with the atmospheric aspect, we're dealing with spirit. The Kingdom of Earth vibrates on a certain level. The atmospheric aspect of the earth when we engage that and know that God wants us to be fruitful, and subdue, and multiply.

There are three layers of the atmosphere of the Earth surrounding the earth

The Earth's principalities, its powers, and its wicked spirits rule the three layers of atmospheres. Everywhere you go in the atmosphere, you can feel it sometimes. If you have developed your ability to sense and to feel and to pay attention, you can feel the principalities, or you can feel the powers, or you can feel the wicked spirits.

Oftentimes we see people's behavior and think they are wicked. But it's not them; it's just wicked spirits doing things. But when we see into the realm of God's Kingdom, we are seers. We know what is going on. We are aware.

The tree of knowledge

Adam and Eve were forbidden to eat from the tree of knowledge (which was both good and evil). But there was another tree . . . the tree of life . . . that God gave them permission to eat from. When Adam and Eve picked from the tree of knowledge (and knowledge is the operative word), they began to retain what they saw. But they retained more of what was happening around them in the atmosphere, contrary to God's Kingdom.

One of the challenges we face (just like Adam and Eve) is when we are not hosting from within properly. Instead, we implode with realm of responsibility, and the implosion exposes us to the influences of the outside world, and we lose our ability to engage the realm of His government. Adam's body began to control his spirit, which blocked him from his ability to engage. They did something that they knew not to do, and they were veiled from seeing in the realm of the God.

Our soul needs to submit to our spirit

This goes back to the spiritual principle that when God created us as spirit beings, His spirit was hosting our bodies and our souls. Our soul and our body were not hosting His spirit. God was in control.

God blew into Adam and he became living soul; therefore, Adam's body is now hosting the Kingdom of God. It shows that our body is designed to host this realm of the government. It is a clear picture of how we were created to be and how we need our souls to submit to spirit.

But one of the challenges we face when we are not hosting from within properly is that we implode with the realm of possibility. And the implosion exposes us to the influences of the outside, and we lose our ability to engage the realm of His government. Our brain is the only thing that empowers our spirit mind to interact with the natural world, not our body to interact.

Remember, God designed imageries in the Bible that are twofold . . . images in the Spiritual realm we can use while in the earthly realm as a tutor to teach.

The soul animates pictures for your imaging

The soul is the animator . . . kind of like Pixar. Your soul is like a Pixar in that you can animate cartoons. And your soul is the gateway between heaven and earth.

"Seeing imprints the soul."

We are taught by vibration in the Kingdom of Earth

Have you ever noticed that when you yawn while speaking to someone, the other person yawns as well? It had always been a mystery to me, but now I know it's because of vibration.

We feel it first, and then we see it. That's how the realm of God's Kingdom operates. What do I mean by feeling it first and then seeing it? In Genesis is says, "The Spirit of God moved over the face of the waters." There was movement. There was sound. When something moves, you can feel it. The Spirit of God hovered over the face of the water so there was movement. Water carries vibration. We felt it. Only afterward did He say, "Let there be light."

Man's body is about 70% water. The function of water is to carry vibration, and the water holds more information than the outside information.

Our bodies store information as well. It is a listening device and that's important to understand. It's a transmitter filled with energy. In fact, our bodies are an antenna.

I remember coming out of my house and trying to open the gate. I had the control in my hand, I was pressing the button and trying to open the gate, but the gate would not open. One of my friends said, "Put it under your chin and press the button, instead of doing it at the gate, aiming at the gate, and pointing at the gate." And when I did that, the gate automatically opened up. Because my body is a transmitter.

This connects with the Keys of Knowledge.

Change your knowledge to change your vibration

To train your inside man about truth is to allow what's on the inside of you to be connected to two thirds of your brain. When you do that, your body vibrates on a whole different level. When you're training yourself about the truth, that is the keys of knowledge.

The Bible says in the Book of Luke that the Keys of Knowledge is like a fragrance. But fragrance is not about smelling. Fragrance is about frequency.

The Keys of Knowledge is like a fragrance, but the fragrance is about frequency. Remember, that is how we learn . . . through the frequency . . . through vibration.

If you are given an orange to smell, you can smell it, but you don't know what it is. When you are given the knowledge of what it is, then your body creates the frequency to understand that it's an orange. The next time you smell an orange, and you smell it without anyone saying anything about what it is, your body has already registered the smell, you've learned by vibration, and your body knows that it's an orange.

The two thirds of your brain gives you the ability to paint pictures and connect with invisible realms that you've never been connected with, and the keys of knowledge gives you that ability. When you change your knowledge, your body vibrates on a whole new level. When we begin to access and understand the keys of knowledge, which is truth, then the two thirds of our brain has control over the one third of our brain (the conscious brain).

"When you have the keys of knowledge, you know what to do with what you know."

Remember, the principle for that is . . . God teaches you how to retain what you see. And then it accumulates truth as well.

The two powerful forces in Earth

Remember there are two powerful forces in the Earth: the power of a presence and the power of an absence. When you're present, people love you. When you're absent, people miss you.

Chapter Eleven

SECRET SEVEN: THE KINGDOM OF GOD IS WITHIN YOU

"The Kingdom of God is what you profess."

—*Dr. Showalter Johnson*

Now that you understand Jewish culture, have followed the protocols, know how to develop your visionary capacity, and have engaged in the Kingdom of Earth, it's time for the next step. It is time for you to access the Kingdom of God that is within you. And you will witness your inner man come to life.

Remember, your inner man is two-thirds of the brain, and that two-thirds is the Kingdom of God. It is your own court on the inside of you. And the domain on the inside of you is a government.

When you use your inner man, it has the ability to teach you how to see God's realm in you that is not of this world. When you reinforce these teachings by using Godly images to trigger your Godly imagination to access the two-thirds of your brain, everything can be covered.

When we see inside of ourselves, we are highly imaginative as Kingdom citizens. When we use the Word of God to allow images inside, we can overcome the outside man from the inside.

Fallen Eyes and Kingdom Eyes

There's a difference between seeing with fallen eyes and seeing with Kingdom eyes.

Kingdom eyes are when you're seeing in the Kingdom and seeing one thing. It's a picture of the dove. The dove is a picture of purity. It can only see one thing at a time.

Fallen eyes is when you're disjointed.

People who look with fallen eyes are looking for problems, not solutions. They react and respond to their situations rather than being proactive.

That is demons at work. If you go to lunch with a person like that, everything they speak about is always negative or a negative reaction about another person or situation. They are more intrigued with the dark stuff as opposed to the light and the life and the way.

Let go of fallen eyes . . . the words, pronunciation, and phonics that are filled with confusion.

If you see with Kingdom eyes, you are engaged with God. If you see with fallen eyes, you see some of the Kingdom, but then your eyes are dipping into fallen eyes, so your imagination is not relevant to God's Kingdom. You're focusing on more things that are demonic.

Choose instead to create yourself with Kingdom eyes from the inside by practicing the Laws of Zion. By practicing the Laws of Zion, not only are you hosting the domain of God inside of you, but you are learning how to keep charge of the courts of God on the inside of you.

How do you keep His courts inside of you? It's simple. Through practicing the Laws of Zion.

The 12 Laws of Zion

"The laws of Zion help to exercise Kingdom authority through responsibility."

Whenever the word of Zion is mentioned, it is speaking about a place in Jerusalem, but Zion is a marked place and it points inward. The interesting thing about Zion is it is a gate and really speaks about the marked qualities of the Jewish people and the inequalities that distinguish them.

The Laws of Zion are components that, once we practice and incorporate them into our lives, shape the domain of God on the inside and mark us as distinctive... as distinct people, just like the Jews. They are the 12 pathways to take in order to fully develop our inner man.

The operative word is *inward*. Zion speaks about the marked qualities of the Jewish people and the inequalities, but it points to the inside. So, the Kingdom of God is on the inside.

What are some of the signs we can look at to know we are developing the Kingdom of God within us?

When the 12 Laws are formed on the inside of you, it develops your inner man, it creates a sense of responsibility, and a partnership with God.

The 12 Laws reveal that God would like us to rule *with* Him, reign *with* Him, govern *with* Him.

This is the way we walk in the ways of God as it relates to being responsible.

The picture of the twelve foundations in Revelation creates a picture of 12 pathways.

When the Jewish people crossed the river, they crossed in 12 different paths based on their tribe. Each particular tribed had its own path.

We can see that the 12 Laws help us to walk in the ways of the Lord from within, which helps us to create a sense of responsibility to govern with Him.

One of the scriptures, Zachariah 3:7, says if you walk in my ways and keep my laws I will give you charge over my courts and rule . . . and allow you to judge my house and give you a ministry to walk among them.

So, keeping his laws and following his ways. Let's examine those laws to keep and the ways to follow more closely.

1. **Sacrifice.** Sacrifice is about offering our passions and pleasures to God. Sacrifice helps to create a goal for ourselves. The Jewish people are known for sacrifice. The goal is to allow our passion and pleasure to be pointed in the right direction. As we know in the Old Testament, they slaughtered animals before God and placed it on the altar. Today, we must place our animal soul on the altar. That animal soul is a need for power and recognition; we must bind our passion to God's passion and our pleasure to His pleasure.

2. **Harmony.** It is imperative to our harmony as it relates to body, soul, and spirit. For example, a friend of mine was in a car crash. Because of the emotional trauma, she was emotional for years and could not get over it. And because of that, her soul was out of alignment with her body and spirit. Before the trauma there was integration . . . that's where the word integrity comes from. But traumas like divorces, car accidents, losing loved ones . . . that's when we fall out of harmony with our body and spirit.

    People who don't have harmony on the inside of themselves cannot be good seers because their soul is out of alignment. It is left open to be a target of familiar spirits or different things of the past or even witchcraft to come and activate visions in our dreams...which interfere with our Godly images.

But, once we have inner harmony we are on our way. Harmony is beautiful for any person to see in Kingdom realm. After all, God's name is Harmony, shalom . . . and His ring has a signet. The signet is truth. Every king had a ring with the stamp on it. When the signet stamps, it leaves the full mark of the truth, because truth is absolute . . . never half, only full.

But the name of God cannot be stamped all at once. Every day we must do good acts, give to the poor, keep our thoughts lovely and pure, and then we gradually grow into harmony with His truth.

3. **Resonance.** Resonance is the quality in a sound of being deep, full, and reverberating. The Jewish people reverberate memories, stories, learnedness by passing their culture down from one generation to another. There have been many countries and civilizations that have disappeared, but the Jewish people are still here. In their voice lies resonance of deep and right ancient heritage.

4. **Time and Space.** Before we can understand the Kingdom of God, we must understand what seek "first" means. First relates to time. If we are to understand how the Kingdom functions, we must understand time as it relates to this government as well as its calendars and seasons.

Of special importance is understanding the future in the back and the past in the front. That's what you call thinking with the end in mind.

Remember, God creates twice. He created Adam and Eve, image and likeness, which is in His mind was where the future is. And then He comes back in reality and creates them out of the dust. So, we see that the future is in the mind and the past is coming after in reality. So, when we look at time in this way, it will give us a special quality within our life . . . distinctive traits that, when everybody is perceiving past in the back and future in the front, you are going in a different direction. You are perceiving the future to be as the end in mind and the past to be in front as something to be relived.

Remember the importance of visualization . . . just like we discussed when talking about Einstein and downloading images before bed. Studies show that many people use this strategy for projects. And what happens when they think of the end in mind, they visualize what they want, and that visualization becomes the model. And, then they relive that they're living and it's what they already thought about.

That shift in time allows you to develop your ideas and visions and things that you want to do in your life to become successful. So that inequality with time changes everything with time and space.

Let's look at it in another way. There is a model . . . vision from the end . . . and in all of us we are made in Christ's image and likeness. So, we have images of who Christ is . . . visions that are locked up in the inside of us. That's already in our minds, and that's already been given to us.

Unfortunately, what happens when we tap into other imageries and visions is those shape our lives. But the original images that have been given to us are the blueprint and framework for our lives. Once we see that . . . the original images . . . then we walk in those images that we're seeing.

5. **Creation.** The law of creation explains the concept of the world being made from nothing into something. It also explains the concept that God continues to speak to the world by telling it to exist. Once he stops doing this, it goes back to nothing.

Creation also explains that the work is being recreated every second. These principles are used to help us exercise Kingdom authority in our lives.

6. **Lordship.** Lordship is where a lord governs mandates. Lordship connects to the word landlord, so landlord speaks about owner. But lordship to God is He owns everything, but we, who are His ambassadors, don't own anything. The Bible says that He owns the cattle on a thousand hills while we only have access to what the Father owns. So that is a unique quality that helps to shape the Kingdom of God on the inside and that defies private ownership, because private ownership creates competition.

Many people today are beginning to find out that access is much more powerful than private ownership. As a matter of fact, it is becoming much more expensive to own . . . to own a house or to own a car. Look at the success of things like Uber and Lyft and Airbnb and community gardens and shared childcare among mothers and fathers. So, you are seeing people beginning to collaborate and share, and, once they collaborate and share, they discover life is much easier.

So, the principle of Lordship is to access territories, but not own them. To access territories from our Father and through collaboration we make things easier for each other.

7. **Kingship.** A king releases mandates. The Kingship model is all about ruling . . . it's not about following the rule, it's about leading the rule. Scripture says in Genesis that Adam had dominion over everything . . . meaning that he led the rule. He was leading it; he didn't follow it. Following the rule only took place when man fell, because they picked from the tree of knowledge of good and evil. That tree was symbolic to another

rule of pharaoh, which is the oppressor. So, when man began to follow the rule, they fell from their place of authority.

So, the thing about Kingship is to find out our sphere of responsibility on the inside of us . . . whatever God has called us to . . . and to lead the rule.

8. **Sonship.** Sonship is about a picture of a small cow being yoked to a big cow. The small cow will follow in the big cow's footsteps and learn how to plow. But then there is a time when the small cow becomes big and breaks the yoke that's around its neck. This is a picture of true Sonship . . . that we are the little brothers, and Christ is the big brother and when we are bound to him, we develop true sonship.

9. **Legislation.** The ability to legislate the judicial laws that are the 12 Laws of Jerusalem on behalf of God (which you will learn about in Secret Eight). Every government has laws made by its government. Remember, in the Kingdom government, you don't own anything, you only have access to what the king owns. This same principle not only enforces sharing, but also shows that private ownership is a deception.

For example, a woman told me that she owns a house and she paid it off in full. I asked her if she still paid property taxes. She said yes. I asked her if she were to stop paying the taxes for a while, what she thought would happen to her house. She said they would take the house away. I said that's my point . . . in the Kingdom we only have access to what the Father owns. We own nothing.

10. **Trading.** Another word for trading is marketplace. The Bible says that the Kingdom of Heaven is like children playing in the marketplace. Marketplace means trading floor—we are all trading, sowing, and reaping and that serves as a very

good example of how we trade spiritually. So, the trading floors we see in New York or Wall Street or wherever came from scriptures in the Bible. And that's one of the things that distinguish the Jews; they deal with a lot of trading in their society, so that's a powerful law.

11. **Wisdom.** Wisdom is the application of the facts you receive in life. That is another internal distinctive quality to help to develop the domain of God. Wisdom nourishes these things on the inside. Solomon doesn't act for money first, he acts for wisdom first.

   Wisdom is a pure nonverbal thought that exists inside of you. It's always in principle form (principle form meaning a seed), and the seed is called wisdom. It has value within itself. Wisdom equips you for position and teaches you how to judge and bring justice.

12. **Chancellorship.** A Chancellor is a legal official or a presiding judge of a chancery court. But in the Kingdom of God, there's a treasury there . . . there are angels there.

Those are the 12 laws of Zion that are aligned with the Kingdom of God. Once we apply and practice the 12 components to shape the Kingdom of God on the inside of us, the Kingdom of Heaven comes upon us and great things begin to happen. The Kingdom of Heaven is looking for something like itself, and these 12 laws of Zion really help to develop that on the inside.

Once you master these 12 Laws, that means you are a good host of God's domain inside of you. You've used creative triggers, Godly images, and pictures to trigger your imagination. Now you're ready for the Kingdom of Heaven, which is God's domain outside of you. When you are a good host, that spills out. You go into the Kingdom of Heaven.

Chapter Twelve

SECRET EIGHT: ACCESS THE KINGDOM OF HEAVEN AND IMPACT EVERYTHING THAT SURROUNDS YOU

External is reality; internal is spiritual.

—Dr. Showalter Johnson

You've been a good host of God's domain on the inside of you, and now you're ready for the Kingdom of Heaven, which is God's atmospheric domain outside of you.

Once the believer is finished exercising the principles found in the 12 Laws of Zion from within, this gives the believer responsibility and authority in their life. Now the believer must exercise the 12 Laws of Jerusalem from without, which helps them to act upon their responsibility in their dominion. They can now preside because they have responsibility and a relationship with God, and they know how to walk in the ways of the Lord.

Remember, there is a difference between existence and life. Because if you can't understand that what is inside of you is existence and what is outside of you is life, then dealing with the inside of you is irrelevant.

The Kingdom of God exists within you. Kingdom of God deals with getting things to exist from nothing. Kingdom of God shapes your existence and develops you for the next level. The next level is the Kingdom of Heaven which deals with life outside of you.

When you get to the Kingdom of Heaven, you become like a person of life. It's traversing with the outside . . . the effect that you have on your surroundings.

That's what the Kingdom of Heaven is all about . . . how you affect your surroundings is what we're really here for; that is, to make a change in society. Who doesn't grow up wishing they could change the world? Who wouldn't like to do their part in the Kingdom today? The Kingdom of Heaven is how it's done.

Existence and living is a duality. We know that Kingdom of God wants to exist on the inside of us, but, once it's developed, the Kingdom of God wants to be validated and opened up into something else. That existence is taking up space inside, and it wants to be validated because it has existence. Growing and learning the Kingdom of Heaven is the way to validate your existence through life.

That's the real power to create life and affect your surroundings. You affect your surroundings in that realm as a seer. That's when you know you've been into the higher realm, because you become equipped to affect the surroundings around you, such as Judicial matters if that is God's kingly anointing for you. But it's anything that may be a problem for a person or a nation that you're willing to affect by what you speak and what you do.

There is a conflict between existence and life on the outside, too. That's the longing someone feels after they shape the 12 Laws of Zion on the inside. It's on the inside taking up space, but it doesn't want to stay there. It wants out to be validated. Like a person who is wealthy and affluent . . . now his existence wants to be validated, but too often that person chooses outward validation through things and attention and celebrity. But that person can easily go into depression . . . we've seen many instances in recent memory of celebrity suicides. I suspect that their existence wanted to be validated still, regardless of all their earthly fame and fortune. But if you develop the Kingdom of God inside of you, it's the same thing, only different. That question mark about existence and life is going to be in your spirit. And that is how you can deal with life and balance your life.

Interesting Facts about the Kingdom of Heaven

- The Kingdom of Heaven shows how to legislate on the outside in the affairs of nations.
- The Kingdom of Heaven functions like a marketplace.
- The Kingdom of Heaven is what you possess.
- It demonstrates how to judge and expedite cases and affairs on behalf of God.
- You can legislate from where you are.
- The Kingdom of Heaven is about You and Me.
- It's God's domain on the outside of us.
- The Kingdom of Heaven is like a mustard seed.

Keys of Binding

What are the keys of binding? They connect to God's atmospheric domain outside of you which gives you access to the Kingdom of Heaven. What principles do you need to know if you have fears and are going through a process where you want to declare that you are ready for the Kingdom of Heaven?

The Bible says in the book of Matthew, "I will give you the keys to the Kingdom of Heaven, and whatever you bind on earth shall be bound in heaven." And the keys of binding connect with the Kingdom of Heaven only.

Look at the rich image found in the story of Elijah and Elisha. Elijah is the big brother. Elisha is the small brother. Elisha saw Elijah plowing with 12 yokes of oxen. That yoke of oxen is the picture of binding. It is another rich image for us to see.

Elisha leaves what he is doing so that he can bind himself to Elijah. As long as Elisha was by himself, he was yoking himself to different things that perhaps did not serve him well. Yes, he was plowing in the soil and doing good. It was still natural, but he needed a reference. Elisha needed guidance and schooling. So, he followed Elijah for years, and whatever Elijah did, Elisha did. He yoked himself to Elijah because Elijah was the blueprint. Elisha followed him and binded himself to him, and then began to access whatever was on Elijah's life.

That's how to use the keys of binding. When God says, "I will give you the keys of the Kingdom of Heaven," the keys to the Kingdom of Heaven is binding.

Jesus and the Keys of Binding

So, we can see the image of big brother, small brother type of modeling in the book of Matthew. Even more clear is that Jesus is our big brother. The little brother is us. Jesus is our model and our blueprint. When we are yoked to him, then wherever he goes, we follow.

Keys of binding is used in the principle of follow leadership when Jesus says, "Follow me." Follow means actually to assist. When you see the principle of binding again, you see the whole concept of the big cow as model, small cow as follower. As the big cow walks, small cow follows and becomes the shadow. The big cow is the overshadower. Small cow is the shadow, and so everything is now locked in, and they become one. Remember, whatever we see, we are transformed into. There's alchemy that takes place. That's the keys of binding. That's how we tune and tap into his domain on the outside of us.

The Marketplace

When the Bible speaks about the Kingdom of Heaven is like children playing in the marketplace, liken means function. The Kingdom of Heaven functions like a marketplace. The Kingdom of Heaven always speaks to finance and the economy.

The Kingdom of Heaven means the mansions of the Lord. In the mansions of the Lord, there are treasuries and angels. In the Bible, we see that the Kingdom of Heaven is like a woman sweeping and looking for a lost coin. That woman who's sweeping looking for the lost coin is saying that, in the Kingdom of Heaven, you can access certain things and find answers in God's domain. That's a domain that we can access.

When it says the Kingdom of Heaven is like a marketplace, God's marketplace can nurture us. When it says the Kingdom of Heaven is like children playing in the marketplace, there's actually an atmosphere that we can experience . . . the marketplaces of the Lord. There are certain things that we need in our life to be effective ambassadors for God's Kingdom, and so we need to be nurtured.

How will the Kingdom of Heaven come upon us once we have been a good domain?

It's really the same principles of binding with the big brother, small brother.

The big brother wants the small brother to be bound to him. Then, whatever things in the small brother's life that's out of character drops off, and he becomes the same mold and the same shape as the big brother. He becomes formidable to the big brother. The big brother is looking for a shadow of itself. That's what happened, so the Kingdom of Heaven is actually a model and is looking for a shadow of itself. That's why it says, "He who dwells in the secret place of the most high." That's way up there. That's the Kingdom of Heaven. "Shall abide under ... " Under means the Kingdom of God, what's on the inside of us.

The Kingdom of Heaven Must See Something Like Itself

Once what's on the inside of us is abiding under the Kingdom of Heaven, then the Kingdom of Heaven can interlock and can come upon us because it sees someone that looks like itself. That's why we have to go through those protocols with the Kingdom of God, which is being a good host of God's domain on the inside of us and forming that existence on the inside of us. Once that is done, then the Kingdom of Heaven sees something like itself and it comes upon us.

The Kingdom of Heaven is at Hand

When the Kingdom of Heaven comes upon us we have access to so many different things. When the Bible says, "The Kingdom of Heaven is at hand," it means that it is very close to us.

The Jewish people saw the hand as a function, not just a form. It was seen as something that covers and nurtures. The hand was also seen as a tree that nurtures. So, when the Bible says, "The Kingdom of Heaven is at hand," the Kingdom of Heaven is like a covering for us that nurtures our life whenever we walk into certain domains outside that correspond with our anointing. When the Kingdom of Heaven comes upon us, it's like God's covering over us that is also nurturing our life.

When that happens, it means we are seated in our sphere of responsibility. Scripture says we are seated at the right hand of the Father. You see the word hand there, and you see the Kingdom of Heaven is at hand. The hand also means full provision. God nurtures us in the domain that exists outside of us.

The hand of the Kingdom of Heaven is a domain that is there to cover and nurture you, and the full provision is there for you. His marketplace is there for you. That coin is there for you. The pearl is there for you. The farmers are there for you. The growth of a mustard seed is there for you. But that special domain comes upon you only when you begin to really understand what's going on.

The Kingdom of Heaven is like two farmers. It speaks about nurturing and growing things.

The Kingdom of Heaven is like a mustard seed. It speaks about exponential growth and how things grow.

The Kingdom of Heaven is like a merchant, a person who knows how to trade and do business.

The Kingdom of Heaven is like a pearl, which is a God commodity.

All of these things, when you download the imagery and understand the parables in the Bible, are really saying that the Kingdom of Heaven is ready to provide things that can nurture our lives.

Become Seated at the Right Hand of the Father

When we are seated in high places at the right hand of the Father, we are in our sphere of influence and seat of authority. God then covers us and allows things to come upon us.

It is unfortunate that most people today are not in their seat of authority. They have not picked up their responsibility, for whatever reason . . . whether it's because they cannot see, or because of what they've been taught, or because they hope and pray that God does the job for them. They want God to do everything for them. But seated at the right hand is about discipline. The hand of God nurturing and comforting you means you have shown a sense of discipline.

Let's talk about Elijah again, so we can see how we activate the seer's kingly anointing. Elijah is praying for rain as a prophet. There is recession in the land, so the economy is in shambles, and Elijah takes it upon himself to pray for rain. But because of his intercession, Elijah had to do something first.

Elijah interceded. He prayed and prayed, and he was a great host for the Kingdom of God. Because of that, automatically a hand appeared. It was a cloud in the form of a hand. When we look at the scripture, we see two things . . . a cloud and then a hand. Because we are now seers, we can tap into that and understand what's going on. The hand there showed up over Israel because it needed to be nurtured. Remember, the hand is a function . . . it means a tree, and a tree is all about nurturing.

So, Israel was in a recession, and the hand came. We see that message in scripture as "The Kingdom of Heaven is at hand." That hand was a prophetic picture to say that God is there. Where? In God's atmospheric domain that is outside of you. So, look . . . it's about to rain. That shows an abundance that is about to come over Israel because of Elijah hosting the domain of God. Because God saw a great host, He saw something that looked like itself and showed it in the form of a hand. That was a prophetic sign, and it came over the people, and then it began to rain. Whatever was in lack, full provision came for Israel, and Israel became the right hand.

Then the Kingdom of Heaven really came upon the people. Taking it into these metaphors and using these rich pictures show people how the Kingdom of Heaven comes upon us.

How will it come upon me after I'm finished learning about, seeing, and activating my visionary ability and being a good host? How will I get to the Kingdom of Heaven? What is the how? A lot of people write books, but they never give the how. That hand, like I said, is all about the full provision of God. It is all about covering, discipline, and comfort.

The Kingdom of Heaven suffers violence

When God speaks, he speaks in questions. Why is the Kingdom of Heaven suffering violence? When scripture says, "The Kingdom of Heaven suffers violence, but the violent take it back by force." Again, in the book of Ezekiel, the Bible says that violence had been found in Satan.

What does that really mean when it speaks about violence there? We know violence from a natural standpoint, but we don't know the word violence like the Hebrews do. When violence was found in Satan, it really meant that Satan took a carbon copy of the seed line into a different realm. In other words, when he was falling from heaven, Satan was very busy with cross pollination of genealogies and seed lines. That's why the same individuals we know that were on David's team were actually giants.

They were from the Anakim race in the town of Gaza and Gath and were rejected by everyone because they were cross pollinated. It's similar in today's earthly realm, when you see people rejecting children with special needs or innate physical problems. They tend to be rejected. In the same way, these giant soldiers who were with David were rejected by people. The giants were cross pollinated. So the Bible speaks about what violence really is. It is taking a carbon copy of a seed line into a different realm, borrowing traits, and borrowing features. What Satan did was take the genealogy of these giants, and their genealogy was not flawless.

Take it by force

The genealogies of a lot of prophets are not flawless because somewhere back in their roots, whatever they were seeing was commingled with the demonic . . . not only spirits but people. As citizens in God's Kingdom, we have to take God's domain back by force and take it back by authority. We are unable to do that if we haven't already been a good host for the Kingdom of God on the inside of us.

As we know, David was a king who had soldiers. David understood his kingship anointing. Kings are all about plundering and going off the spoils. By worshipping in the cave and playing the harp, David changed the DNA of these men. Later on in the word of God, they became judges in the book of Israel. This shows us again that we learn everything by frequency and vibration. Our relationship with God is what allows us to take back by force. That was a way that David was able to take it back by force, based on his intimacy with God and the soldiers being in his presence.

Remember I said whatever you see a person do, you are transformed? They saw what David did, and they became transformed. That is another way of how to take things back by force . . . by doing whatever the Father tells us to do. That's one of the ways we take it back by force, but another thing that really suffers violence is a lot of the inheritances and economies. A lot of things suffer it. So we must take it back by violence.

You take it back by force by doing what David did and by doing what you see your Father do. You take it back. You transect the affairs of nations. You take it back by force through colonization.

Elijah, who was a powerful prophet, goes into a place that was not compatible with what he is saying. If I'm a prophet and sent to a certain territory, most people would say, "I want to go to a territory that is going to receive exactly what I say." But that would be easy, and that's not how you take it back by force. That's not how Kingdom prophets do it. You are sometimes sent to a place that is not compatible with what you're going to say to them.

When I tell people that, they will say, "Well, God is not a God of confusion." In their minds, they think that wherever the prophet goes, he is going to say something that everyone believes, and they're going to agree, but no. That's not it. When you are sent, you are sent into a place that is not compatible with what you are saying. So, you have to speak it. And when you speak it, you will overthrow whatever is happening there. You colonize. Colonization means you come in with a certain type of influence, and your influence invades the territory. Then your influence really establishes ground.

Another way of looking at taking it by force is to transect like infection. Transect means that when I come into a territory with the word, the territory may not agree with what I'm saying, but I transform them. I transect them by what I'm saying, and they catch what I'm saying. What I say becomes the norm.

If we think that wherever we're going to be sent means everyone will agree with what we say, then we are not looking to do as He says and take it back by force. Taking it back by force is changing the DNA of that person through colonization, through invading the territory with your influence and showing the way. You have to be a good host of the Kingdom of God inside of you first so that when you enter into the territory, the influence of what you carry is felt, and then you can overthrow what is there.

Enter a domain with God's anointing for you

If the Kingdom of Heaven is actually a domain, it's very important to be seated at the right hand when we're seated. That's where we're covered and disciplined . . . because we are seated in our purpose and our assignment.

When you have full provision, nothing can be lacking out of your life. If we look at a chart, for example, you have first the priestly, secondly you have the kingly, and then you have the sphere.

Priestly anointing

When we look at the life of Joseph, his priestly anointing was that of a prophet. He was a prophet because he was able to see first things in vision and dreams. Then the second thing he did was communicate. He sees it in the Kingdom realm. Then second of all, he communicates that to the king, so this communication is not coming from hearing the voice of God. His communication came by seeing God himself in his Kingdom realm. When they communicated, they didn't communicate it because he heard God saying it. They communicated because he saw God doing it.

Kingly anointing

Remember, the kingly anointing is a role of government. Joseph's kingly anointing as a prime minister was to solve problems. If the Kingdom of God is the government, then each of us has a role of governmental responsibility that we are called to operate in. You see the role of government in all of the lives of the prophets in the Bible.

Joseph's kingly anointing as a prime minister and his sphere of influence in government and business is how he is seated at the right hand of the Father. When he understood his priestly, his kingly, and the sphere of influence that he is called to, then he is seated at the right hand of the father.

What is your kingly call? How do you use that for the glory of God?

What is your kingly call? What is your sphere of influence? How are you going to take the nation back by force? Your kingly anointing from within is all about something special that you can unleash.

First you must remember kingship and that it's a sacred law. Kingship is about releasing mandates that have not yet been unleashed into the earth. There is something that you have been called to do that carries your thumbprint. Therefore, only *you* can unleash it in the earth.

Let's examine the roles of Daniel, Deborah, David, and Moses. By studying these figures in the Bible and understanding the meanings of the parables, you will know the secret of how to be seated at the right hand of the father. You will know your seat of responsibility and be covered and nurtured to practice your anointing . . . wherever you may be.

Daniel was a prophet, which was his priestly anointing. He saw things, and then he communicated what he saw. His kingly anointing was that of governor. And his sphere of influence was government. He was called to government.

Deborah also had a priestly call as a prophet. Her job was to see things and then communicate to the court as a magistrate. Being a magistrate was her kingly call. Her sphere of influence was government, just like Daniel.

David's priestly anointing was as a prophet. He had an ability to see and then communicate the word of God, but his kingly anointing was a king. Which means his sphere of influence was called to government.

We go to Moses. His priestly anointing was a prophet. He was called to see and communicate the Word of God, but his kingly anointing was a lawyer. He wrote the Ten Commandments. His sphere of influence was what? Government.

There we see the common theme . . . a kingly anointing in government.

Which anointing should you use when you enter a territory?

How do you fulfill your destiny in the earth? What's the protocol?

If you are a person with a priestly anointing of prophet and also have a kingly anointing, how do you determine which one to use when you enter into a territory?

Again, we are discussing protocols. I've seen people who have entered into certain territories and try to enter in first as a prophet. But the most important thing to understand is that God is wanting us to unleash our arena of government, which is God on the inside of us first. You must know that before anything else. When you enter into a region, you enter in with your kingly anointing first.

Once you do, the Kingdom of Heaven comes upon us and great things begin to happen because it is looking for something like itself. Just like a mirror. You become the mirror.

The 12 Laws of Jerusalem

"The Laws of Jerusalem helps to exercise Kingdom authority relationally."

The 12 Laws of Jerusalem are designed for us to be able to deal with life situations . . . meaning the effect we have on your surroundings when we are called to the affairs of nations.

The 12 Laws of Jerusalem are used in prayer and should be seen as judicial laws that affects everything within the environment that we live in. Once we realize that these laws can be used in prayer to bring justice on earth, then we are presiding in prayer over the affairs of mankind, changing seasons, ruling, and governing with God. The image of the law is Jerusalem.

Jerusalem is a house

Jerusalem functions as a spiritual center for the world. Not only that, it has to judge and expedite a spiritual external mandate from its city. So, Jerusalem can be envisioned as a house.

And the 12 Laws of Jerusalem represent the principles for the external mandates and God's timetable for the Kingdom of Heaven. Those principles are:

1. Judgment (begins on Feb 2th for 70 days)
2. Justice (second 70 days)
3. Grace (third 70 days)
4. Mercy (fourth 70 days)
5. Spirit and Life
6. Sin and Death
7. Love
8. Faith
9. Sowing and reaping
10. First born
11. Abundance
12. Righteousness

How to legislate using the calendar

How do we legislate these laws of Jerusalem? From February 2nd for 280 days, four sets of 70 days correspond with Judgment, Justice, Grace, and Mercy. During each 70-day period, that particular law is in our favor in the courts in earth and in heaven. The remaining 85 days in the calendar are used to legislate for Spirit and Life, Sin and Death, Love, Faith, Sowing and Reaping, First Born, Abundance, and Righteousness.

Remember, God creates twice . . . the court in earth and the court in heaven. God makes these laws available to us to use in the spiritual realm of the courts to decree over wills, inheritances, misdeeds, divorce, property, etc.

Judgment, the judicial law from Jerusalem connected to the first 70 days of the courts, gives a sense of discernment. If people have experienced wrongs in their life, the law of judgment is in your favor then.

I am a legislator. It's an inner quality that I produce and carry to legislate spiritually. I can speak and decree as a king over the lives of many people who experience injustice. I can decree that the courts of heaven are saying: listen, from February 20th to 70 days afterward, judgment is in your favor. The court is ruling in judgment that whatever was taken from you is going to be given back.

I used my kingly anointing as a legislator to help a woman who had a lot of property taken away from her. I watched as she lived through her situation. Remember, as a seer, watching means from the seer's realm. Remember what we discussed in Secret Five about vision following a progression? There's a difference between seeing and watching and there's a difference with looking.

Daniel 14 v 17 said: "I watched as a watcher." Watcher really means an angel. So, when you watch something, you're watching how something moves in the spiritual realm.

If I open the curtain and I see it, then I see it. I opened the curtain and saw something. There's nothing I could do not to see it, unless I closed my eyes. Then there's looking. If I'm looking at the newspaper, then I am intentionally doing it. But when I'm watching something . . . like a movie . . . like the legislative calendar . . . I'm watching because it's moving from one scene to the next.

So, when I'm watching something it is because I can . . . I'm using my seer's ability in different realms. If I see one thing, that's one level of the anointing. If I look, that's another. And when I watch, it is another level. It is the highest level. You can have the legislation qualities inside of you, but the secret is knowing how to allow them to spill out of me. That's what the Kingdom of Heaven is . . . it's knowing how to use it to affect your surroundings.

Judgment

When I preside over cases such as the woman's, I'm able to tell her that, in the courts of heaven, February 20th to 70 days afterward deals completely with judgment. Which really means that I am watching the days and months go by on her behalf. The same way those months are moving in the realm of the spirit, as a prophet and seer I could watch things change over her court case at the same time I was watching it. I was watching that judgment was going to come in her favor.

Justice

Now after those 70 days are over, the next 70 days in the courts of heaven is Justice. So, what happens with anyone who I'm praying for or any court cases with property or wills, for example, as a watcher I can watch over those 70 days. As I do, I make decrees over that person's life. And I legislate as a judge, and I speak and decree . . .

this second set of judicial laws means whatever you've been dealing with, justice is going to be on your side.

Grace

A third set of 70 days is then grace.

Mercy

And another set of 70 days is mercy.

Spirit and Life, Sin and Death, Love, Faith, Sowing and Reaping, First Born, Abundance, and Righteousness

These remaining eight Laws of Jerusalem are left over to be used to expedite externally to intrude in the affairs of men who you are trying to help. Those are the laws of spirit life in effect. So, for the next 85 days in the courts of heaven, those eight laws are in effect, and they are marinating together. It's almost like a garden that bears fruit. But then the garden needs to take a rest in order to revitalize itself. And that's how the courts of heaven are . . . it's almost like this garden.

How can I as a Kingdom citizen preside from a spiritual standpoint?

Remember, Biblical figures were legislators. Moses was a lawyer, Samuel was a judge, Daniel was a governor, Deborah was a magistrate, and Joseph was a prime minister . . . just to name a few. Your responsibility is to bring that ancient wisdom into today's time and give it meaning for how to legislate.

Remember, not to legislate from an earthly standpoint such as a legal attorney. We have been called to legislate on behalf of God as judges, legislators, chancellors, and kings. We are to judge with a sense of discernment, not brimstones and fire. We must use discernment to help people in the earthly realm.

So, the courts of heaven, just like in earth, has a courtroom in the Kingdom of Heaven. That's how you preside as a Kingdom citizen from a spiritual standpoint.

If you're appraising property, you have to appraise correctly with the correct measurements. What is the strategic positioning of the house? The strategic positioning is always external. So, when you're judging His house, you are literally saying I'm judging the house of the Lord so that God can intervene into the affairs of man and into the affairs of nations.

We are the kings. We legislate those things. We are the chancellors. We have the wisdom to do it. We have the trading to do it. We have the sonship to do it because we are mature. We have the time and space because we perceive future and past differently than everybody. We have harmony within ourselves and we have to sacrifice to do it. The Kingdom of God has shaped us, and the Kingdom of Heaven has come upon us. Now we can judge His courts and keep His house.

How are you going to judge His house?

"Rule my house and judge my courts."

We find this statement in the Bible in Zachariah. Two words are very important . . . I will allow you to rule my <u>house</u> and judge my <u>courts</u>. Two words that comprise courthouse. Zacharia 3 v 7 says walk in my ways, keep my laws, and I will allow you to judge my house (Jerusalem) and rule my courts (internal).

If I'm going to keep his court, then I already understand the Kingdom of God inside of me and the 12 Laws of Zion. If I'm going to judge his house, I'm going to appraise these laws of mercy and justice and know what law connects with certain days in the courts of heavens. Then I speak and decree as a king on behalf of God. Then

God interferes and intrudes into the affairs of man in the natural realm and brings the deliverance upon their life.

That is the how you be a keeper of the courts and how you judge His house. I call it the courthouse anointing, which is a special anointing that God has given me. I speak it differently, and it is Jewish. It's right there in the scripture . . . we just have to look.

The Beth Din

And remember how we do this? The Beth Din. The Jewish court of law composed of three judges who were the very wise apostles responsible for matters of religious law and settlement of civil disputes. Remember, the operative word is three. The Beth Din explains the structure of how to judge the court systems. The three is so important because it means to be caught up in the heavenly supply. When Paul says I was caught up in the third heaven, the three there means the heavenly supply.

The Beth Din also means house of judgment. So that goes back to Zachariah 3 v 7 . . . you can judge my house. This is what He promised to those who seek his government and to His ambassadors who understand his Kingdom.

The court system used to be coordinated by the church. Today it is separated, and so there is dichotomy. The church structure dealt with three types of disputes . . . marriage, divorce, and inheritance disputes; and the three judges, the Beth Din, dealt with those.

So, what would the Beth Din do? In order for them to judge the house, they needed to know how to legislate the 12 Laws of Jerusalem because they had to deal with external human matters. Marriage cases needed mercy or grace or judgment or justice. And they needed these judgments not from the natural court, but from a higher spiritual court.

So, the Beth Din would sit on behalf of God. The natural court couldn't deal with these matters because they would've had to go by what they see. There needed to be a higher judicial law, and the rabbis would rightly discern and decipher through the spirit what was going on, and they would select one of the 12 Laws of Jerusalem that would be connected to a case.

Let's say someone needed mercy. That means if you did something wrong, you really need the mercy of God to correct things. There are a lot of people who've made mistakes in their life, and they turned their life around, but their past is still being judged. So, they have to go before the court. Natural courts would not understand certain things. But these judges knew which of the 12 Laws of Jerusalem . . . in this case mercy . . . to select in the case.

Another might need grace. Another might need justice. The Beth Din knew how to discern because they had the inner qualities of the 12 Laws of Zion as prerequisites inside of them to give them the ability to adjudicate over court systems in Israel. And if they didn't have those qualities, they would not be selected to do that.

Be like the mustard seed

Always remember that the mustard seed imagery is like the Kingdom of Heaven. The mustard seed is a Godly image of abundance and how it changes its surroundings through nurturing and covering. When it is planted, the mustard seed is very small, but grows over six feet tall. It provides shelter as covering and roots and seeds for nurturing. And when the blows, it picks up the seeds, plants them again elsewhere, and spreads abundance for its surroundings once again.

Chapter Thirteen

SECRET NINE: GOD NEEDS YOU

"The person who is before you does not control your destiny. The person who is in you controls your destiny."

—*Dr. Showalter Johnson*

Knowing this secret enables you to change your life and the lives of others forever. It enables you to take on your responsibility to partner with God and change the seasons and surroundings of your life. It is not for me or you to get on our knees and pray and ask Him to do it for us. It is up to us to partner with Him as an ambassador with our kingly anointing.

So, you've reached the Kingdom of Heaven level. You govern yourself and are a good host of the Kingdom of God with the 12 Laws of Zion inside of you. The Kingdom of Heaven sees something like itself and comes upon you. You now see the 12 Laws of Jerusalem as principles that you can use to be a change agent. You have the tools you need to invade cultures in need of these 12 principles. This is what it means to act on behalf of the affairs of nations. That's a strong principle of what it means to be a king, because kings invade.

The 12 Laws of Jerusalem represent the 12 different ways that a seer can use to bring life to his surroundings. Yes, that is, to invade and bring change and life to your surroundings as a partner and ambassador of God. That's what God needs you to do.

Just like Daniel.

Daniel said he had visions of the courtroom in heaven. So, when he had a vision of the courtroom in heaven, he sat silent in the court. He watched the 24 elders and he saw books being open. The book has pages that look like scrolls, and there were pre-chapter and post-chapters.

The pre-chapter detailed certain assignments that have been attached to many people before the foundations of the world. The post-chapter in the book deals with all of the mistakes and failures that a person would have made after they were sent into the world. The post-chapter shows that even in our mistakes, afterward God forgives us and we have a chance to come before him. All we are required to do is repent as we come before his courts, knowing that because he still loves us even after (that is, post) our mistakes, we still have a chance to be restored because all of these things have all been working together for our good.

Think about how rich that looks. Whatever the Bible says of Daniel seeing a courtroom in heaven, that is seeing in a spiritual realm. That shows us that *we* can imagine that, and that *we* can tap into it. There is certainly a courtroom in the earthly realm, too. This shows us even further that whatever we are seeing on earth was actually in heaven first. And that shows us that everything on earth got its blueprint from heaven.

Daniel saw that rich courtroom. So how does that rich image allow us to trigger our imagination? We can go there. We can go to that place. We can go there by accessing the Kingdom of God within us. We can see it, and then we can go there.

The courtroom is just one example of life and how you can affect your surroundings. The life of fire is not the same as water . . . even though they exist in the same way. That's the same principle with the Kingdom of Heaven teaching you about life and how you affect your surroundings. There are myriad things in your surroundings that you can affect. Just like water and fire are different, so is the government in each of us and our sphere of influence.

If your sphere of influence is the courtroom, use the example of Daniel to deal with court cases here in earth. Use the legislative calendar for guidance with God's timeline. You can go to the spiritual realm to deal with those situations. A court system is filled with so many things that need the life of so many individuals to positively change the lives of people and their children.

I've been to the spiritual realm using my keys of binding so that I could impact court cases here in earth. One of the first times was when I was in South Africa where I went into a certain region to work as a business consultant to help a company start a non-profit mutual company that would use fresh approaches to mentor young business leaders. An envious man was slandering my name and saying untrue things about me.

What I did was remember that Daniel saw a vision of the courtroom. That vision had to be real, but it was not of this world. It was in the Kingdom of God. It was the world in me. Recognizing that I could use imageries from the Bible to practice my creative ability and my Godly imagination, I downloaded it. I studied it. I triggered my imagination with Daniel's vision of the courtroom. About 15 times in a row before I went to bed. On the 16th night, I went to sleep. And while I was sleeping, a visitation of angels came for me to take me to that same courtroom. I'm in the courtroom, and I'm before the court, and the angel teaches me what I needed to know about how to deal with my enemy.

The book that I saw was similar to the one Daniel saw. The angel would tear a page out of the book and serve that scroll to the individuals in earth who have forgotten their call and assignment in the world. The scroll would also be served to those with kingdom assignments to be served to the enemies of those people. In the seer's realm of the kingdom, this is called "serving principality papers."

The judge was there, and I had six big golden keys. The angel said, "You will only use one key today." I asked which key. He said, "You will use the keys of binding." Then I started to speak in the court, saying "I know binding is a legal term." But the angel rebuked my thoughts of what legal binding was, and he said, "If you bind the devil to yourself, then your nature will become formidable with the devil's nature. Even more confusion would then be produced in your life. Everything you try to pronounce would bring death and confusion." He was teaching me how to re-work it, and then he said, "This is what you do. You bind to your rabbi, which is the ancient of days," and so I did that. I started to bind.

Then the angel told me the person in Africa who had been working against me is only a subject to the adversary, and the adversary is in the courtroom today. I said, "Who bears the adversary?" He said, "See him there, he is the prosecutor. The devil in the Kingdom is actually the prosecutor, and Jesus needs them on his board."

The angel reminded me that in every government there is opposition. In the United States, there are Democrats and there are the Republicans. You always need an opposing force inside the White House, or inside the senate, or wherever. He said, "The devil is the prosecutor. Stop giving him power in your life because we are not creating any more demons."

The angel said they have no creative ability or authority. He said, "Bind yourself right now to your chief rabbi, to your nature, and follow him; and whatever is on his life in heaven is going to come on your life in earth."

That morning, when I went back to the meeting with my enemy, that person's attitude toward me was completely different. That was what I was able to bring about. I was able to use the courtroom as an image, use my keys there, and come back to earth. My body vibrated on a different vibration because of what I had learned. And their countenance toward me changed completely.

It changed everything for me. Before I went into the spirit realm and interacted with that Godly image, I had been binding the devils in me and allowing his life and his nature to bring deception and confusion in my life. I was going in the opposite direction. The angel said that, when I used the keys of binding in reverse, I hid the door. It was very difficult to find. It was upside down. But I needed to bring it back up to the position it needed to be, and I accessed the Kingdom of God in that realm.

It was a responsibility that I needed to take. It wasn't someone else's responsibility. It's not the matter of fact of who was before me. Who is in me and who is in you is the king, is God, the Kingdom of God, and is a responsibility that we all have. God gives me that responsibility to partner with Him to change seasons in my life, not for me to get on my knees and pray and ask Him to do it for me. My duty is to partner with Him as an ambassador. That picture from Daniel was a way to trigger my creativity and allow me to enter into the courtroom of God, but not just a courtroom, but to enter into the courtroom with keys.

We must learn how to create a picture in our heads, so we don't forget. That way, we don't have to see it to see it. And that's just what I did. I created a picture in my head, so I didn't have to see it to see it. And I impacted my surroundings.

Using the Laws of Jerusalem

There are a wide range of situations where a person who needs to go to court. Let's say they go to court because they want something that belongs to them. But the judge rules against them, and the judgment wasn't right. The 12 Laws of Jerusalem show the different types of people and times that people need to have God's law rule in their favor. Each one of the 12 Laws of Jerusalem teaches the seer how to affect life and surroundings in 12 different ways.

Let's look at a few more examples.

Grace

Grace means that which you cannot do, so God is going to have to do it for you. When you know you're not qualified for something, that's when you need a higher power to take precedence in your life. Grace can affect your surroundings even though something may be not in your favor, because grace spoken and understood teaches you how to bring life.

Abundance

Abundance is another principle in the Kingdom of Heaven of how you bring life...and the image is as simple as a mustard seed. As we have discussed, a mustard seed is very small, but becomes about six feet tall. Its leaves grow which in turn creates a place for the animals of the field and the birds in the tree. Its roots provide nourishment for the strawberries, and the wind blows and the seeds grow elsewhere, and the process happens again. That is abundance that changes surroundings.

Love

Love is another law that you can use to affect your surroundings and those of the people around you. Recently I visited a boy who wanted to commit suicide because he thought of killing a young girl. The courts sent him to a mental institution where it was fierce and destructive and filled with many rapists, criminals, and dangerous people of all sorts. But when I went inside to see him, he was watching "Winnie the Pooh." I was struck by this dichotomy.

I asked, "Did anyone come to see you?"

He said, "Yes. The pastor of our church came."

"What did the pastor say?"

"God loves you."

"How do you feel about that?" I asked.

"A bunch of crap; a bunch of b.s. Why, what do you think?"

I said, "I agree with you."

"Huh?"

"I agree with you that God does not love you."

He said, "What's your point?"

"God needs you," I said. "God doesn't love you because he needs you. He needs you because he loves you."

I understand where love belongs in a sentence. If love is misplaced in a sentence, then it is misplaced in our surroundings. Therefore, if love is misplaced in our sentences, then love is misplaced as a thought in our existence. That means it's misplaced outside of us . . . out of life. We're using love not to effect change, but using it to operate in reverse.

So, the boy thought God was looking at him. But "I love you" is self-love. That's you loving something for what you can get from it. But if you say you *are* loved, love can't love itself. Love is a means to an end. Love cannot maintain itself.

I told the young man that God recognized God needs you, not loves you. I saw that the boy felt a sense of being needed and necessary...maybe for the first time in his life.

He said, "I'm not going to kill myself anymore because God needs me."

This conversation shows why people shoot strangers and cause such harm . . . they don't feel needed and recognized. When we use Love as a Law of Jerusalem, we know it shifts the environment and surroundings. In a culture or system that is deep with hatred . . . use love.

Justice

How many people need justice? During the financial crisis of 2008, there was no justice for those who committed fraudulent activity in order to distribute huge mortgages and high interest credit cards when they knew people weren't qualified and wouldn't be able to pay for those things. So many people lost their homes and their financial security.

Bring life to your surroundings

Most people don't know how to bring life to their surroundings. They can only bring existence. And mere existence breeds depression.

So, how do we embellish instead . . . how can we change our lives . . . how can we continue to move?

The most important thing to understand is, as a seer, you begin to see elements and environments and life and everything operating around you through a magnifying glass.

Remember, with the 12 Laws of Jerusalem you're dealing with abstract laws that are not touchable, but they can change and influence. Now you want to look at the environment you *can* touch . . . like the wind that blows the leaf . . . that's coming to help you make decisions now.

It's one thing to use the 12 laws to help spiritually invade cultures to change for the good, but now it gets to a point where you leave your home, and everything you see is taking up space, yet *they are all on a timetable.*

I was spending time with my son. I said, "This is a chair. Now, I place a cup on the chair. If God speaks and says to the chair to move, where will the cup end up?"

My son said the cup will fall to the floor.

So, I asked him another question. "If God said to this chair now put the cup back on it, and then God says disappear and go to the balcony, what will happen to the cup?"

He said the cup will fall to the floor.

That's our disbelief of understanding how God works.

If God speaks to the chair to move, the cup does not move . . . it stays suspended in air because he never spoke to the cup to move.

Everything is on a timetable. That's important for seers to know when they get to this level.

When the leaf drops, it doesn't drop on its own, God told it to drop.

When it blows across the road, the wind isn't blowing the leaf . . . it's actually God telling the wind to blow the leaf.

So, everything that is happening is existing, but life is always going on around us as we speak. And it's always giving us signs and signals about the divine will of God and the new things he wants to show us about what we need to do.

You see this in Divine Providence.

I know a woman who was in her house and started having thoughts about a friend she hadn't seen in years. She left her house to go to the grocery store, and she saw her friend. That was Divine Providence.

There was a young student of mine who told me about a dream she had about her friend who was scheduled to take a plane flight in three days. The dream was about a bird falling in the plane and fog covering the windows. When she told me about the dream, I advised her to tell her friend to reconsider taking that flight. The following day, her friend went to pick up her ticket. Her friend heard someone speaking about an engine and how the engine was leaking oil or some type of fluid, and they needed to fix it. The next day, she told me her friend went to a Starbucks where she overheard someone else talking about fixing planes. Her friend overheard those types of conversations three times in a row before her flight.

Whenever you see three things happening in row it is a touch of Divine Providence. It is a symbol to alert you or give direction to unknown answers. What it's trying to do is use things outside of yourself in nature to speak to you directly about a decision you need to make. This demonstrates that even though the Divine Providence of God is always moving, God wants us to be a part of understanding seasons and symbols, but too often our own thoughts that govern our life cause us to miss out on what God is showing us.

In this lady's case, the decision was about flying. I told her to tell her friend not to go on the flight because she's been getting signs. The plane will crash.

It is very sad that my student was not obedient to my instruction and missed an opportunity to share this alert with her friend. The plane did crash, and her friend died.

We discussed the principle of engaging the elements around us. The heavens are always declaring. Things are always declaring the glory of God. One thing is declared . . . it's an image . . . you're seeing it . . . and the image forms.

Nature is outside of us, but if we don't know how to see, then we are blind. When we don't understand the timetable and what we're seeing, we cannot use the laws correctly.

What happens when people choose not to see at this seer's level is that something prohibits them from seeing, and it's called the "human soul." The human soul is based on the underlying thoughts and beliefs based on how we're brought up and how we grew up. Those thoughts become limiting. Sometimes we see elements, but we do not follow intuition. Because the human soul is limited by how we think of ourselves, it becomes limiting to the problems and challenges we have in life.

The God soul is overriding whenever we see two or three things that look alike. Three blue cars, three 7s, three things with 5 in it . . . that's the Divine Providence speaking through the God soul and the will and the magnetic attraction of things.

A seer needs to know what the will is which is an electric magnetic attraction of things.

If you, dear reader, don't know how to be a seer, you are going to miss the God soul. I got you on my timetable. It is your season and time. Instead of opening up because you cannot see, you make a bad decision and that door of awareness is shut. That's what causes too many people to miss the timetable.

Don't let that be you.

"Can you see it?"

Chapter Fourteen

Mateo rose from his bed filled with an excitement he'd not felt in a long time. Not since his journey of discovery finished, in fact. That was the last time he knew with certainty what he had found, what he had found out, and the great message he wanted to share with the world.

But that excitement had long passed years ago, for his message fell on deaf ears. He went to the prophets who couldn't explain what he saw before . . . as if to make them see the truth. His intentions were fine and good. But the prophets still shook their heads. Or had a different explanation to tell him that he now knew wasn't true. When he tried talking with people outside of the church, they too looked at him with bewilderment. Some even laughed at him.

He had decided he must not be adequate to share the message, and that he had failed in some way. So, he spent the next few years writing his discovery down lest it be forgotten. He didn't really know how he was going to use the pages he wrote. He just knew they came to him and down through fingers as he typed at his computer . . . just like when his fingers touched the keys of a piano.

He drove to the church in a bit of a rush, jumped from his car, and ran inside the church, waiting for Evan to return. He stared out the windows and watched the waves slam the shore and the tourists line the beaches.

And then he saw Evan, running toward the church . . . just like Mateo had done moments before.

Evan burst through the open door . . . holding Mateo's pages to his chest and his guitar out to his side. He stopped when he saw Mateo and tried to catch his breath.

"I take it you liked it?" Mateo laughed, while noticing that the young man's face glowed with new wisdom, and his eyes danced with excitement.

"You gotta tell people about this!" Evan said.

"I think I just did."

"No man, not just me. These are the answers I've been looking for. No one ever believed me."

Evan set the pages on top of the piano bench, leaned his guitar against the frame, and turned to Mateo.

Evan opened his mouth to speak, but he found no words. Mateo extended his hand to shake Evan's, but Evan embraced Mateo instead. The laughter and tears of both of them were mingled. They felt validated and understood for the first time.

For whatever reason, Mateo sat down on his bench. Evan picked up his guitar. And the two played . . . the most beautiful rendition of "Secret Place" anyone has ever heard.

Suddenly Ledija opened the big wooden door and stepped into the church. She saw the two men playing and laughing. She knew what she saw was pure joy and did not interrupt, but instead was lulled into the music's beauty.

After the last notes resonated throughout the church, once again Mateo and Evan locked eyes and laughed again. Mateo placed one hand on the pages and one hand on Evan's shoulder.

"Excuse me," Ledija said.

Her voice startled both of them.

"Oh, yes," Mateo rose from his bench and went to her with an outstretched hand. She took his hand, and then placed her other hand on top.

"You were right! You were right!"

She threw her arms around Mateo and tears rolled down her cheeks.

"You saved my life. The doctor said I had a blocked artery. He said I came just in time. He said I could've died within a month if I hadn't come in to see him!"

She pulled herself back from Mateo and looked in his eyes.

"How did you know?"

Evan laughed.

"I just did. I saw it," Mateo said, simply.

Evan picked up the pages from the piano and held them out to Ledija.

"These explain how he knew," he said.

She read the title, "The Nine Secrets to the Seer's Realm of the Kingdom" out loud.

"What's this?" she asked.

"It's the story of how I came to find out how a seer can see . . . to help people discover the seer's realm . . . of the Kingdom," Mateo said modestly.

"Oh," she said, flipping through the pages.

"So, this tells you how to do it?"

Mateo nodded.

She looked at Evan.

"And you can see things like this, too?"

Evan nodded, glanced at Mateo, and put his arm around his shoulder. For the first time in their lives, these two men . . . from different parts of the world . . . knew how it felt to be believed and seen.

"Do either of you have an agent?" Ledija pulled out her business card and handed it to Mateo. "Because I know a good one."

"You need to share these secrets with the world."

www.ingramcontent.com/pod-product-compliance
Lightning Source LLC
LaVergne TN
LVHW091225080426
835509LV00009B/1176